Seven Faces of Darkness

Seven Faces of Darkness

Practical Typhonian Magic

Don Webb

Vol 1: Proceedings of the
Order of Setne Khamuast

Rûna-Raven Press
1996

Visit Our Website at:
www.seekthemystery.com

Published by
LODESTAR
P.O. Box 16
Bastrop, Texas 78602

This small scroll brings word of the Word of the winged secret flame and is dedicated to the Griffin of the West, who holds Osiris in his paws, the Eye of the South, who moves freely through the Earth, Baal of the East, who strikes as Set, the Risen One of the North, who holds this Scroll; Ra-En-Set, who took up the Word in our time; Arabis, who dwells by the springs of Python; and Na'amah Anath, who is my Sekhem.

Acknowledgments:

I am indebted to all the scholars who have helped Open the Door of the South. Special thanks are due Dr. Ann Macy Roth, Dr. Edward N. O'Neil, Dr. Stephen E. Flowers, James Graeb, Leon Wild, and Dr. Phillipe Derchain.

The Toolbox that Walks like a Book

It is the curse and the blessing of humanity to exist simultaneously in two worlds: that of the tangible real and that of the intangible ethereal. Unlike all other animals we are not content with physical life's sensations; despite sober argument and methodical science we never quite believe that "this is all there is" to our existence. We are drawn, some gently, as in fantasy and dream, some more insistently and passionately, — to something *else*, something *greater*, something that lifts our being and our significance *clear out of nature*, far beyond the realms of atoms and molecules: a magnificent mælstrom of gods and daemons for whom "reality" is but a poor crutch for brutes on the periphery of their much larger universe.

If the mystic is content to dream about this other universe and the artist to convey glimpses of it in music, paint, or pen, it is the passion of the magician to *interact* with it. The magician seeks to draw its presence and power into the lesser world, to change that world by its touch.

The magician fumbles at this. There are no ordinary tools Here that he can reliably apply There, and the great rays of the gods that flow so inexorably and thrillingly through "nature" are just as elusive. They are to be glimpsed out of the corner of one's eye, unexpectedly. The magician struggles to fashion new and different tools for control which he, in his semblance as sentient, natural man-beast, can use reliably and repeatedly, as one would use a wrench or hammer.

To non-magicians his efforts my appear bewildering, even foolish. They are illogical. They don't make sense. They are but "melted into thin air." Perhaps they are even harmful in that they entice others into the same useless folly, draining energy which might better be put to serious, practical labor. The magician may thus find himself ignored as an irrelevant eccentric, perhaps even ostracized as someone dangerously insane.

Yet he continues with his great work, his search for tools. Sometimes he thinks he has indeed found or fashioned just such a different kind of wrench or hammer, and he writes down descriptions of it and instructions for its use. Sometimes other magicians, in their quest for tools, come across what he has written and try his ideas for themselves. And sometimes they indeed seem to work, and so another brick has been added to the bridge between Here and There.

Don Webb, a magician, presents you with some tools of many ancient magicians which he has tried and found to work. Don

Webb, a scholar, also wants you to know something about the history of these tools and those who first fashioned them, because he considers such contextual knowledge vital to their design and application. Don Webb is pretty good at explaining all this in the language of this side of the bridge.

Michael A. Aquino

Table of Contents

Chapter 1
Why This Book Came Into Being

Indeed, magical spells are divulged, oracles and the spells
of meeting and seeking are made dangerous because they
are remembered by men.

Admonitions of Ipuwer

I've wandered between two camps all my life. One is the
camp of practicing occultists, people who seek to use magic as a
way of exploring and manipulating the world, but who shun
logic, research, and precision. The other camp is the camp of the
scholar who values precision and research, but fears to actually
put into practice the methods they discover. My encounter with
the Word of Stephen Edred Flowers convinced me that a practical
synthesis of the two camps could be achieved, as well as
suggested to me a practical methodology for such a synthesis.
With the best scholarly sources I could find, I began a study of
the god Set-Typhon, one of the most frequently appearing figures
in the magical papyri of Thebes and whose name is found in
curse tablets around the Mediterranean.

Set-Typhon drew my attention for several reasons. The
Egyptian god Set, who represented a fierce separateness — an
individual drive for power and knowledge — was largely a
suppressed "forbidden" deity of the Egyptians. He had been a
patron of the pharaohs of the XIXth and XXth dynasties. I was
curious why this god had (then as now) a remanifestation, and
why he was coupled with a Greek monster. Why did literate,
well-educated men of late antiquity come to this particular
synthesis? It seemed at best unlikely.

As I began to answer these questions, I discovered deeper
cultural and historical realities ranging from hitherto unexplored
aspects of the survival of Egyptian practices, to the discovery of
attitudes toward magic and philosophy that impacted my own
becoming. I would like to share the beginnings of my
understanding of Set-Typhon in the Hermetic tradition, so that
others may make use of tools I've found and of the method of
discovery.

The majority of operant texts available to us come from the
third to fifth centuries of the Common Era. Most were found in
Thebes, a collection whose history and whose magical and cultural

1

significance has generally been overlooked. This key collection, which escaped the Roman persecution of magical texts, can be tied in with similar spells on curse tablets found around the Mediterranean. The practices of the Theban library are the key to a widespread magical/philosophical view of the universe which shaped the thought of Late Antiquity, and which in a Hidden manner have shaped and are reshaping magical practices of the twentieth century.

What I wish to do in this book is examine the papyri and tablets, the Egyptian contribution to the papyri, the Greek contribution. Then on a more operative level, I wish to show the postmodern magician how he or she may use this technology, its presence in the world, and sources to deepen his or her understanding. The most perceptive of my readers will see this entire Work as a demonstration of method, which they may use to rewin whatever mysteries the world holds for them, whether it be Mayan sorcery, the Oghams, or the intricacies of the Tao.

The process I used in reconstructing the darker operant side of Hermeticism was a threefold process which I initially read of in a paper by Dr. Flowers with special emphasis on the semiotic model of magic.‡ I feel that the process has been valuable in both personal transformation as well as giving me clear results through the activation of existing scholarly material. I think the process that Dr. Flowers has developed has the potential of changing the way we do both magic and scholarship in our world, and is of special significance at this time of ideational shift. The process is one of objective analysis, followed by subjective synthesis, and finally enactment. Let's examine the phases.

Objective analysis. If I wish to re-create the practices of others, the first place to start is the hard facts. I am fortunate at the wealth of operant material available to me, the papyri and tablets. Likewise a surprising number of primary texts dealing with the illustrative magic of Hermeticism have survived, such as the *Enneads* of Plotinus or the *Hermetica* (Scott, 1993). These primary texts combined with the archaeological and historical records available give us an accurate picture of what these magicians did — not only in the material sense, but in terms of their social and linguistic milieus.

The latter material is necessary to discover how these individuals perceived *the order of their worlds*. Magic, the art of changing the subjective universe in order to produce a

---

‡ "How to be a Heathen" printed in *Idunna* IV:4 (December, 1992), pp. 11-16.

2

proportionate change in the objective universe depending on the passion and precision of the operator, begins with a received world view (though by necessity this world view individuates with the practice of magic). For an understanding of the world view, as many factors as can be handled by the reconstructionist should be taken into account. If you want to make the same journey as the original operators, you must start as close to the same place as they started as you can, and you must arrive at the same destination. In determining the destination, which must by necessity be individual given the nature of magic, we do have the popular accounts of the lives of practicing Hermeticists. Indeed such accounts may have already shaped our minds about the nature of magicians; the popular Greek novels of late antiquity had a strong effect on Goethe's *Faust* and the emergence of the magic story in modern times.

This emphasis on objective data gathering is also an emphasis on *self-reliance*. The current magical practice of relying on the channelings or revelations of others bespeak a spiritual laziness. Rather than seeking out the beginning and ending points, many prefer to take the half-cooked models of another individual's mind — an individual who may or may not have achieved that transformation of magic.

It might be argued that the magician who does not engage in objective analysis and merely creates his or her own system is more self-reliant than the researcher. However, the totally self-created system will rarely challenge your blind spots, rarely present you with mysteries to be solved, rarely present you with confirmation that you're on the right track. The difficult process of seeking the objective data allows you in a very real way to remanifest the way of learning that various successful schools have possessed. This may not provide the entertainment of spending a weekend listening to someone channel a kazillion-year-old Lemurian, but it will provide you with one of the closest things available to time travel. The last chapter of this book provides the dedicated seeker some resources if they wish to make the journey I have.

Subjective synthesis. The Hermetic tradition is above all a tradition of individualism, the Setian current within it particularly so. Once adequate research has begun, questions arise that can only be answered by relating the process to the understanding of the individual. A model, as appropriate to Hermes god of communication as it is to current linguistic thinking, emerges. Having considered the traditions under which the model factually

3

developed through time (diachronically), how does the individual make use of it in the here and now (synchronically)?

Having learned the language, what do you choose to say?

An example would be the common practice of dream-sending, an important tool in the Setian toolkit. The questions as to the *meanings* and *ethics* are many. Each individual must come up with her or his own answers as I did. The process of discovery has a twofold thrust. Firstly, it lets you observe, test, and articulate what is hidden in your personality. Secondly, applying your personality to the external tradition then allows you to take a facet of the tradition into your sphere of being. You have claimed it for your subjective universe. Once again, you are repeating the process of the writers of the papyri, and like them using this process to lead to an individual enlightenment.

The actions of my subjective synthesis will not appear directly in this book. But since I realize that I have transformed myself through the use of these techniques, I am aware that the transformation will effect what I emphasize and point out. In this way I am become an authentic teacher/student of this tradition. If you wish a similar position, you must apply these steps. Then you will *know* what is true, not because you read it in my book, but because your soul has discovered it for itself.

Enactment. The magical practices of the papyri are geared for practicality — whether to gain "women and gold" or the answers to the toughest of the soul's questions. The test for understanding a practical system comes from doing. One doesn't read computer manuals for their prose, nor study surgery for amusement. The test of understanding is in getting results.

Only when the circuit becomes self-sustaining have you obtained the goals of the system. When you have changed the subjective universe, produced the change in the objective, and then integrated the new fact into the subjective have you obtained to magic. Then you have taken the dry bones of the past and made it into a living system that enables you to communicate with the hidden secret side of the universe. When you achieve results, you have Opened the Mouths of the Gods.

A distillation of the above threefold system could be contained in the Egyptian sentence *Ir shti shta-(t)u!* ıp barʇ barᴛⱥʏ which could be translated variously as "Inquire of the books of magic!" or "Seek the Mysteries!" or "Travel through difficult territory!" The Egyptian word *shta-tu* may have been etymologically connected with certain forms of the name of Set. By the time of the magical papyri the words meaning "belonging to Set" or "of the secret place" had coalesced in the common

4

tongue. The Egyptians associated certain night sky features with Set, particularly the constellation *Ursa Major* and the planet Mercury. They called Mercury *Sbq* which simply means "the Unknown."

This book came into being for what would seem to be two reasons to the non-initiate, but two sides of the same reason for the initiate. The open side of the reason is that well known phenomenon that in order to understand one's synthesis, one must teach. This is the aspect which led the illustrative writers of *Hermetica* to put down their ideas after having gained initiation by learning to perform the operations of the papyri successfully. The hidden side is that in order to achieve the goal of the "Setian Hermetica," of Becoming a god while still alive — you must Open your own Mouth, as the god Set did for all the gods of ancient Egypt.

In *The Book of Coming Forth by Day*, the afterlife book of the Osiris cult, there is an interesting confession of the good followers of Osiris:

> *I have come hither to see thy beauty, my hands raised in praise of thy true name ... If I enter the secret seat, I speak with Set... but if One veils his face when his glance falls upon secret things, he may enter the house of Osiris and see the secret things that are therein.*

This book is not for the pious who would veil their gaze, and trust to have secret things revealed to them in a later life. It is for those who would seek after the hidden things now. It is not for those who would come forth by daylight to see what is revealed by the light of another, but for those who would come forth by night and see by their own self-created light.

Chapter 2
History of the Papyri and Tablets

Let the Earth be still and the sea be still and the winds be still — and not be a hindrance to my prophecy. No loud cries, no hissing, no sound for I am about to say the Dread Name.

PGM VII.321-325

I. History and Content of the Papyri

The Magical Papyri of Thebes have an interesting history in how they originally came to be, were later rediscovered, and eventually affected the modern occult and academic worlds. The term "Magical Papyri" is limited in this book to mean those papyri from Greco-Roman Egypt whose extant texts date from the fourth century BCE to the fifth century CE. These include texts in Greek and Demotic with glosses and insertions in Coptic and even Hieratic.

This section of my book will deal with the texts, particularly as products of Greco-Roman Egypt. The following chapters will consider them as products of Egyptian and Greek traditions. The majority of the texts were produced after 330 CE when the imperial support for Egyptian temples ended, and — as persecution and suppression increased — the texts became very scarce after 400 CE; although the latest existing text was a horoscope cast concerning a birth in 478, from Oxyrhynchos, a Set-worshipping nome in Upper Egypt. The chapter on remanifestations will show what and how the tradition continued.

Since the time of Prince Setne Khaumuast, Egyptian priests had been in the custom of keeping a working magical library at specific temples such as the Ramseseum in Thebes (indeed the Theban caché may represent the last magical library of Thebes). The lector priest might divide his time half a year working for the god (*sems-neter*), in other words as a servant in the temple; and half his year working-as-the-god (*paχer-neter*), or combine both practices at once. The scrolls belonged to the temple, but were loaned out to the priests, possibly rented out. Magical knowledge was considered a state and cultural resource, but when state patronage died — magic became an individual resource. Postmodern magicians, who often find themselves taking on the burden of maintaining culture and personal power in an increasingly chaotic world, are very much in the same situation as the writers of the papyri.

7

The scrolls of working spells were very much part of his stock-in-trade, and unlike the religious practice — which tended to be highly conservative — the working magician (then as now) would take in any effective knowledge that could increase his power (and earning potential). Indeed many of the foreign words which begin appearing in the New Kingdom make their first appearance as parts of spells or medical recipes. Egypt being perceived as the heart of Order — foreign magic was the best way to introduce Chaos. This preference for foreign words is why ethnic Egyptians *preferred* Greek for "words of power." The Greek Titan Typhon, who was ever plotting to return to the center of the world and seize power from Zeus, was the perfect symbol of such magical desires. Despite the verbal identification there seems to be little of Typhon's myth or form in the resulting deity. (Set-Typhon may be an ironic response to the Ptolemy's Sarapis.)

With the ending of imperial patronage the priesthood of Egypt turned more and more to the practice of itinerant wonder-working (this is made clear by the sudden diffusion of Egyptian names and magical techniques into Europe and Asia Minor appearing in the late fourth century). This class of working magician was not welcomed by Roman rulers.

Roman attempts to suppress magic (and foreign religious practice) were frequent. Emperors passing laws against magic included Augustus, Tiberius, Claudius, Nero, Vitellius, Vespasian, Domitran, Marcus Aurelius, Constantine, Constantius, Volentinian, and Theodosius.

The Roman practice of burning the magical books along with their possessor made the practice of magic dangerous, but Roman decrees did not end magical practices. Only the coming of Christianity, which anathemized all pagan practice, led to the near elimination of all magical practices.

As the combined forces of Roman imperialism and Christian law entered Lower Egypt, heretics and practitioners fled south. The stoning of Hypatia in 415 CE fundamentally destroyed the Alexandrian intellectual community. The magicians of Thebes chose a *deliberate* burial of the papyri. It had always been an Egyptian practice to bury *damaged* papyri with their priestly owners — but the great caché of intact texts from Thebes suggests that something else was going on.

Interestingly a wealthy collector assembled a collection of Coptic Gnostic texts — including also some Greek philosophical texts and medical texts translated into Coptic — from *all over* Egypt, as can be seen from the different languages and scribal

8

styles. This collector carefully had these scrolls buried in the place called P'Vau (the Souls) where the Ali brothers from Nag Hammadi dug them up in 1945. Both sets of texts were deliberately collected and preserved. Thebes, which had held the world's first magical library — the Ramseseum of Setne Khamuast — became the last resting place of the magical knowledge of Egypt.

The authors of the papyri were bilingual in Greek and an already-archaic Egyptian Demotic. The magical consequences of bilingualism is discussed below. The papyri include not only magic (which shows a familiarity with Ethiopian, Samaritan, and even Babylonian magical/religious systems), but also with pharmacology, metal working, and fragments from Greek novels. Intertextually the papyri authors were familiar with St. Paul, religious traditions of the Hebrews, Persian mystery religions, Homer and Plato. Fragments from the mysteries of the Idean Dactyls appear as well as the Delphic maxim "Know Thyself." In short, the authors were learned men familiar with the cultural matrix of the Mediterranean — somewhat different than the nineteenth century view of sorcerers as stupid practitioners of bad science.

The writers of the papyri had a particular interest in *getting things done* (i.e., changing the world or themselves). This led to an attraction to such gods who had power appropriate to their interests. First and foremost Hermes, a logical choice for people often making their living as translators (Greek 'ερμηνης), secondly to Set-Typhon as god of the foreigners (clearly the ruler of the age), and to other sources of foreign power such as Jehovah or Mithras. This identification with a cultural bad boy as a source of power is probably the first example of "Satanism." This active choice of an antinomian figure for self-empowerment coupled with the multi-cultural learning has been without parallel until recent times.

After the Theban documents were cached, they remained hidden for over 1300 years. The interest in things Egyptian made the ancient Theban trade of treasure seeker and tomb robber a popular one. Relics, art, and scrolls were dug up (and manufactured) for the European trade.

The premier collector was Jean d'Anastasi (1780-1857), an Armenian who became the Swedish consul at Alexandria. Anastasi purchased the papyri in Thebes and sold them off to the British National Museum, the Bibleothèque National and the Louvre in Paris, Stastliche Museum in Berlin, and Rijksmuseum in Leiden. The translations of the Greek and Demotic texts had differing effects and histories. Let's consider the Demotic first.

The Demotic papyrus of London and Leiden was a long sheet (16.5 feet) cut in two and sold separately (to Leiden in 1828 and London in 1857). The Leiden text was a key source for the decipherment of Demotic because of the numerous glosses in Graeco-Coptic characters. It provided Brugsch most of the material for his *Demotic Grammar* published in 1855, and was used for translating its other half. The sharp-eyed Pleyte discovered that the two fragments were one, leading to the publication in a single volume as early as 1892. A popular English edition, *The Demotic Magical Papyri of London and Leiden* by F. I. Griffith and Herbert Thompson appeared in 1904 (and has been a popular Dover reprint as *The Leiden Papyrus* since 1974). An amusing side stop for the Demotic papyri was the American horror writer H. P. Lovecraft, who used the odd spelling of the Demotic to cook up the names Yog-Sothoth and Nyralathotep. Lovecraft owned (or at least cited) *Papyrus Anastasi I* in his Commonplace Book in 1926.

The definitive collection and translation of the four Theban Demotic papyri appeared as part of *The Greek Magical Papyri in Translation* edited by Hans Dieter Betz and published in 1976. The Demotic section was edited by Janet H. Johnson (and all numbering of the *Papyri Demoticae Magicae [PDM]* refer to that volume).

The Greek material was much slower in attracting interest. The idea of "magical" didn't fit with the nineteenth century notions of Greeks. The illustrative side of the Hermetic tradition, best shown in Plotinus' *Enneads* (himself an ethnic Egyptian writing in Greek) might be suitable for study, but the operant side was treated as a poor relation. Only in a postmodern epoch can the two sides be restored.

After some initial work by Dutch and German scholars the first substantial publication was by Charles Wycliffe Goodwin who published *PGM* IV in 1853. It contained the spell "Stele of Jeu the hieroglyphist in his letter." Jeu was a figure well-known to Gnostic Christians — *The First and Second Books of Jeu: or, The Logos According to Mystery* comprised the Bruce Codex, a nineteenth century find in Abyssinia.

This famous invocation deserves a few remarks. It is a formula common to many of the Typhonic workings. Firstly, the god, the Headless One, is invoked. Preisendanz identified the complex figure of the Headless One with Set (*Akephalos* 1926 Leipzig). The Headless One is also identified with the Jewish God, Osiris, Abraxas, and Samaritan gods. Secondly, the magician *becomes* the god. Thirdly, in this deified state the magician does the desired work.

This has an interesting parallel in the Coptic language Bruce Codex. The books consist of an *account* of a journey of rising up through successive Aions (including that ruled by Sethys) and then learning the method by which Aions could be created. The two texts point to a common methodology of rising up to become Set and then creating certain forces to work on the world in accordance with the Magician's Will.

The Wycliff translation caught the attention of Samuel Liddell (MacGregor) Mathers, who added it to the Golden Dawn's repertoire under the name of "The Bornless Ritual for the Invocation of the Higher Genius" complete with Enochian Tablets, Kabbalah, and an interesting mistranslation of Akephalos as "Bornless One." In this dramatic fashion, the ritual is still practiced.

In September of 1900, Aleister Crowley performed the ritual from Wycliff's *Fragment of a Graeco-Egyptian Work Upon Magic.* The ritual had a profound effect upon him, leading to the reception of *The Book of the Law* in 1904. Crowley published his own version of the ritual as *Liber Samekh* during his stay in the Abbey of Thelema.

Interestingly, Florence Farr, a fellow initiate of the Golden Dawn, published sections of the Bruce Codex and its descriptions of Aions as being the *product* of a magician, which led Crowley to the understanding and basis of his work. This is an example of the combining of an illustrative working, *The First and Second Book of Jeu,* and an operative Working of the Typhonic Hermetica. Similar results may be obtained by the postmodern magician.

In 1905 Albrecht Dieterich suggested that all available papyri be collected into a single edition. He had a hard time attracting enthusiasm for the project because magical texts were seen as an affront to the nobility of the classical mind. Dieterich died on May 6, 1908, and a few of his students (particularly Richard Wünsch) took over the project.

Progress was made, but Wünsch and others died during the First World War. Karl Preisendanz began the project anew. He published two volumes, *Papyri Graecae Magicae (PGM)* in 1928 and 1931. A third volume with extensive indices was planned and even reached the galley stage, but World War II stopped the publication.

After Preisendanz's death on April 26, 1968, the publishing firm of Teubner brought out a new edition under the editorship of Albert Henrichs. In 1986 the English-language version appeared under the editorship of Hans Dieter Betz. The numbering of spells found in this volume follows that of Betz.

I don't know if the spells (*in toto*) have been archived in any electronic site; although several spells involving Selene and other Greek figures are said to be available on Compuserve.

II. History of the Tablets

There are over 1500 examples of various types of curse tablets, mainly thin lead sheets, but also in pottery shards, limestone, gemstones, papyrus, wax, and ceramic bowls. The earliest appear around 400 BCE, about the same time as the appearance of the Orphic/Pythagorean grave tablets. Over 600 curse tablets have been found in Greece, making them an important source of the operant Hermetic tradition. The terms *defixiones* (binding spells) or καταδεσμοι (curses) are the technical terms for these items, themselves the final product of a magical process. Of particular interest to us are the tablets of the fourth and fifth centuries CE which show a large number of Egyptian elements — particularly the invocation of Set-Typhon. The widespread placement of these spells in Athens, Rome, Galilee, etc. show that the operant side of the Typhonic Hermetica was well spread in the fourth and fifth centuries.

The choice of lead in Typhonic magic goes beyond its relative cheapness (easily stolen from public water pipes) and ease of handling. In the late antique tradition lead was the material of Osiris' coffin. It was associated with the binding power of Set, an absolute sealing of the activity. From the Greek side of the fence it is the metal of Kronos, the dead god, who is seen as being a powerful figure since he controls all of the sea of time and space. Kronos is invoked occasionally, and like Set-Typhon is an example of an entity associated with because of the power he provides the magician who takes on his form, rather than a prayer-answering god of a popular cult. He is also an outsider *returning* to the center.

The binding tablet had long been a part of Greek practice showing up as early as the fifth century BCE. Plato was aware of a professional class which produced such items for a fee. By the second century CE the tablets are widespread through the Roman world.

There is a great deal of evidence that the tablets were produced according to handbooks, indeed some bear the same invocatory phrases found in the papyri. Some of the papyri explain how to create the tablets. The foreign elements in the tablets show how Egyptian thinking and practitioners came to dominate the "market" and that the papyri were the direct forebears of the European sorcerer's book or grimoire.

Of special note is that a large number of tablets were found in Athens, the intellectual center of late paganism. The Typhonic tradition was well represented there even during the Christian persecutions of 460-560 CE. Ultimately the aggressive stance of the Academy of Athens (as seen in their use of myth — Christians being equated with giants and Titans) led to Justinian closing the Academy in 529 CE about which time the Typhonic tradition went completely into hiding.

The Academy moved to Harran in present-day Turkey and later flourished for awhile under the Moslems, which is how many texts made it into Greek and Syriac. Indeed Al-Masudi visiting the Academy in the tenth century recorded their door knocker's inscription: "He who knows his nature becomes god."

This is possibly the last inscribed tablet directly produced by the Hermetic tradition, and would serve as talisman of understanding for the current Setian revival initiated by Michael Aquino.

III. Language Use and Magic

The choices of language use in the magical papyri were determined by two factors: 1) The social/historical milieu, and 2) magical considerations. Actually the first ultimately had a magical effect, but that will be dealt with in Chapter 6.

The social milieu. The amalgamation of Egyptian and Greek populations had been going on since the time of the Ptolomies. Several ethnic Egyptians such as Manatheo or Plotinus had written their works in fluent Greek, and Greek was the chosen language to export Egyptian ideas in. However, the coming of the Romans, with their standard imperial tactic of divide and conquer, changed all that. Roman occupation, particularly after Septimus Servius' time as governor, developed a policy of emphasizing the Hellenic and repressing the Egyptian aspects of religion, politics, and culture.

By 50 CE the only means for recording things for most Egyptians was Greek. Religious and literary texts (being products of the temples) remained in Demotic. But with the ending of the imperial stipend for temples, Demotic came to be used only in magical documents. The Demotic texts were clearly the product of the disfranchised priestly class intended as preservative and/or link to the magical and philosophical Egyptian past.

Other Demotic texts survive, and what makes them particularly interesting is the evidence of a *common* tradition, but different applications. Both Greek and Demotic texts contain identical strings of invocations. The Demotic texts on the whole are prone to the use of substances such as donkey blood, the head of an ass — whereas the Greek texts are somewhat less organic. There are fewer references to Set-Typhon in the Demotic texts. Perhaps one could communicate to the god of foreigners in a "learned" tongue better. One of the three spells analyzed in this chapter had instructions in Demotic but the invocation was written in Greek. In fact it is one of the few Greek invocations embedded in otherwise Demotic writing.

The Greek language provided something for the Egyptian magician that would have been part of a priestly tradition — *vowels*. The operative backbone of Egyptian magic had been far too sacred to write down, but with the decline of priestly training what was once best preserved in oral lore was now best preserved in writing. Although we may presume a near equivalence of sound with the Greek vowels, we must also be aware that Greek *ideas* came along with their vowels. For a full understanding of the Hellenic stream, see *Hermetic Magic* by Stephen E. Flowers. Coptic was very seldom used by the Hermeticist. It seemed the language for *religious* texts, but lacked the power and focus needed for magical operations. Only two spells in this volume — "The Red Cloth of Nepthys" and the spell for oil from a Coptic grimoire — were written in Coptic.

Magical context. One of the most striking aspects of language use in the papyri and tablets is the *voces magicae*. Early theorists of magic tended to dismiss such "abracadabra" as impressive sounding words to frighten or impress those not in "the know." But we are aware that almost all Hermetic magical operations are conducted in secret and alone. Why then the barbarous names?

We can either go with the theories of a contemporary Hermeticist or the postmodern theorists of magic. The Neoplatonic philosopher Iamblichus (writing *circa* 300 CE) writes that the process of theurgy (Egyptian *paχer-netery*) requires the use of foreign terms and magical signs for the theurgist to *receive* the power of the gods. This idea had been established in Egypt by the time of the New Kingdom (as mentioned above). In magical texts from that time, we not only see the use of foreign words, but also the invention of fantastic names. Such exotic names as Hetebteni and Asembeni appear created by metathesis and word association to resemble the words "Terror" and "Protection." Such

14

unfamiliar and artificial names show a desire to find the precise name of the power to be invoked. This long-standing Egyptian practice had a great wealth when blended with Greek ideas of word and sound.

Postmodern theories (beginning with Tambiah in a 1968 essay, "The Magical Power of Words") argues that magical language is not gibberish, but an appropriate form of discourse with another realm of existence. Van Baal (in *Symbols for Communication*, 1971) furthers the argument that the encoded messages are more pleasing to the hidden realms and therefore more likely to produce a response in the form of phenomena. This view of magic is particularly useful for the postmodern magician, who deals in many realities (from her office work to her Initiation) as one of the easiest roads of power.

IV. Analysis of Three Spells

I will examine three spells — two from the papyrus, one in Greek and one in Demotic and Greek; and a spell found on a curse tablet — for language use. This type of analysis is necessary not only for the magician to utilize the given formula but also to allow him or her access to a method of thinking, a recognition of the original material.

Capital letters refer to Greek lower case *voces magicae*. The first spell is a love spell from the papyri. For a fuller analysis of the Greek στοιχια and their meanings, see *Hermetic Magic* by Flowers.

PGM IV.3255-74.
Take an unbaked brick and with a bronze stylus draw an ass running, and on its face "IAÔ IÔ," and on its neck in the shape of a little bell "ÊOÊOÊ," and on its back "LERTHEMINÔ," and on its breast "SABAÔTH," and under its hooves "ABRASAX." Smear it with the blood of Typhon and a pig and with juice of an onion.
The spell of the brick to be written down is this:
"IÔ ERBÊTH IÔ PAKERBÊTH IÔ BOLCHOSÊTH IÔ BOLCHOSÊTH SABAOUM KOKLOTOM PATATHNAX, the shaker, IÔ ERBÊTH APOMPS IAÔTH IABAÔTH SEISAÔ PEUKRÊ, you fortunate one, TESCHÔ PATONAK PHENDE MIEPHEOR ABIRBOLONCHITHI RÔPHTÊ APERMA PALELÔPS, the shaker of the world, I call upon you, great Typhon, IÔ ERBÊTH IÔ PAKERBÊTH IÔ BOLCHOSÊTH, because I am he, (insert magical name of magician). Hear me, in this business

15

which I am performing LERTHEMINÔ AROUZORON BATHOU CHÊASMÊPHIS, O great, great Typhon LERTHEMINO; attend this magical operation which I am performing, because it is your great and honored name that I am saying and writing, ABERAMENTHÔOUTHLERTHEXANAXETHRELTHUOÔENMAREB A.

Write the following words beneath the ass, and then place the brick over the parchment until she comes to you: "Give her the heaving of the sea, total wakefulness of Mendes, and give her the punishments."

Analysis.

The ass is the figure of Set-Typhon in motion. It is named IAÔ IÔ. IAÔ is the common name for the Jewish god in the papyri, but it also refers to the native Egyptian god IAA, an ass-headed manifestation of RE. The name is widely used in the papyri and the binding tablets; it also appears as a cosmic power in the Gnostic texts. By the stoichae its number is 811 (8 + 1 + 1 = 10, the cosmic totality). IAÔ can also be seen as an encoded form of the entire vowel sequence AÊEIOUÔ. IÔ is a common name for Set-Typhon. In the Coptic language IÔ means ass. It is usually found in conjunction with ERBÊTH and other Typhonic names.

The *phallus* and *kestis* symbolism of the bell should be obvious. *Epsilon* is assigned to Venus and *Omicron* is assigned to Mars, and as the donkey runs along there is an alternation of these principles. Note the number of *Epsilon* and *Omicrons* in the *voces magicae* that follow.

LERTHEMINÔ is another Typhonic name keyed to the constellation Virgo. SABAÔTH, the Jewish God but more understood as the Gnostic Demiurge — in other words, like Set-Typhon the Lord of the World. ABRASAX, a Gnostic deity, snake-footed like Typhon, appears in many magical inscriptions. His name adds up to 365, the number of days in the year, and the placement of the running Typhon above him symbolizes that this spells "runs" through time, a common motif in the Typhonic Hermetica playing off of Set's cult title of Set-Heh "Eternal Set" which would also sound like "Set of the Floods."

The phrase "blood of a Typhon" means asses' blood. The ass, pig, and onion all have Typhonic associations. By smearing the *charaktêres* the magician fills them with the presence of Set-Typhon. Modern magicians should of course *not* use blood but should find other substances to produce in them a similar sense of Set-Typhon.

16

The spoken/written spell is a gold mine of Typhonic names as well as interesting examples of the *translation* of Egyptian magical ideas into Greek. ERBÊTH and PAKERBÊTH are common Typhonic names keyed to seven and nine respectively. The latter is found with great frequency in spells to cause love or hate because of the number nine's power to *govern* the minds of men. BOLCHOSÊTH (equal to 986 = 5 which is also the number of SABAÔTH and the principle of Justice) has been decided as the Egyptian pronunciation of Baal, another Semitic deity identified with Set + Cho the Egyptian word to strike, so the name equals Baal who strikes as Set. The shaker is an epithet of Typhon, but also refers to the donkey. The donkey as an alternate form of the Set-animal (see Chapter 3) shares in the Egyptian name for the Set animal — the "beast of destiny" (a name also connected with the pig; see Chapter 3). Set-Typhon is invoked here as a deity who can overturn the natural order.

Note that after all of this invocation the magician says, "I am performing LERTHEMINÔ, etc." In short the magician says that he (or she) is now acting as the god — performing *paχer neter* (literally "reaching the god"). Having transformed *himself* into Set-Typhon the magician then invites Set-Typhon (at this point his other hidden self) to attend and witness the work. The phrase (in Greek) "great, great" is of particular interest. It is an exact parallel of the Egyptian "AA" great repeated twice meaning greatest since the Egyptian lacks comparatives, but translated into Greek rather than using the Greek form of *greatest*.

The palindrome at the end of the formula, clearly identified as the name of Typhon, has a few interesting properties. It begins and ends with Alpha, the power of the moon. This is magic very much in the sphere of this world (sublunar). The elements in their ascent read Moon in Aries (AB), Venus in Capricorn (ER), Moon in Libra (AM), Venus in Scorpio (EN), Name of Toth (TÔUTH), Name of Typhon (LERTHEX), Moon in Air (AN). The force of this incantation is doubled by its backward repetition with reversed elements having the same value. It encodes the process of the spell — raising of desire with goat and ram, appeal to justice with Libra, a piercing of Venus with Scorpio, the name of the god of communication, the name of the god the magician has become, the medium (dreamy night air) through which the message is sent. This particular Typhonic name was also known to Sethian gnostics. Bronze figures of a human-bodied ass-headed Set walking with hieroglyphic gait clad in loin cloth with the pedestal inscription ABERAMENTHÔ (in Coptic) exist. The Gnostic Setians led by Dositheus possessed such bronze

figures, which shows that they were "descended from Seth" —
the figure was much more than just Adam's son. The name is a
form of Montu, a Theban war god whose cult absorbed Set's in
the XXIInd dynasty.

Having transformed him(- or her)self and created the link
through which the message will be sent, the actual message itself
is accomplished in two lines: "Give her the heaving of the sea"
is a standard Typhonic attribute of unrest; "total wakefulness" is a
common form for love spells — not letting the intended sleep
until consummation — "of Mendes" this goat, the Egyptian Bab-
Neb-Tett is a personification of lust "and give her the
punishments" of extreme horniness if not love. (Bab-Neb-Tett of
the papyri became the Baphomet of the *Picatrix*, one of the
earliest Sufi magical texts, and later a figure associated with the
Templars, Oswald Wirth, Eliphas Levi, and Anton Szandor
LaVey.)

The brick weighs down the parchment "holding" the spell in
place, until the intended is drawn to the spot. The practice of
supraposition — putting something on top of something else to
control it — is an Egyptian magical technique from earliest times.

The next spell is partially in Demotic. Demotic material is in
italics, with words of power notably in Greek.
        PDM xiv. 675-94 [*PGM* XIVc. 15-27]
*A spell to cause "evil sleep" to fall. Formula: You bring a
donkey's head; you place it between your feet opposite the sun at
dawn when it is about to rise, opposite it again in the evening
when it is going to set; you anoint your right foot with yellow
ocher of Syria, your left foot with clay, the soles of your feet also;
you place your right hand in front and your left hand behind,
the head being between them; you anoint one of your two hands
with donkey's blood and the two corners of your mouth; and you
recite these writings before the sun at dawn and in the evening
for four days. He sleeps.*

*If you wish to make him die, you should do it for seven
days. If you do its magic, you should bind a thread of palm fiber
to your hand, a piece of male palm fiber to your phallus and
your head. It is very good.*

This spell which you should recite before the sun:
"I call upon you who are in the empty air, you who are
terrible, invisible, almighty, a god of gods, you who cause
destruction and desolation, you who hate a stable household, you
who were driven out of Egypt and have roamed foreign lands,
YEÔUTHUÔEY you who shatter everything and are not defeated.

18

I call upon you, Typhon Set; I command your prophetic powers because I call upon your authoritative name to which you cannot refuse to listen, IÔ ERBÊTH IÔ PAKERBÊTH IÔ BOLCHÔSÊTH IÔ PATATHNAX IÔ SÔRÔ IÔ NEBOUTOSOUALÊTH AKTIÔPHI ERESCHIGAL NEBOUTOSOALÊTH ABERAMENTHÔOUL-ERTHEXANAXETHRELUÔTHENEMAREBA AEMINA (the whole formula). Come to me and go and strike down him, (insert name) (or her, insert her name) with chills and fever. That very person has wronged me and he (or she) has spilled the blood of Typhon in his own (or her own) house. For this reason I am doing this" (add the usual).

This spell's preparation involves manipulating the *physical* form of Set as Ass-headed man, as well as other practices to concentrate the magician's attention. Head, feet, phallus, hands, and mouth are drawn into the process — as well as the whole of the life of the magician as occasioned by the planning and control needed to perform the operation. "Evil sleep" is a nightmare-filled night that begins to destroy the physical and mental health of the victim. Nightmares were considered a special creation of Set from at least the XVIIIth dynasty (when in the *Book of Dreams* it was written that nightmares are "evil filthy things which Set, son of Nut, has made"). The rubrics also encode Neoplatonic number lore. Do something four times to make a change, seven times to make it permanent.

The spoken spell in Greek is interesting both in the rich list of epithets and clues it offers us about *praxis*. At first the spell calls upon Set, and then later the magician prophesies as Set-Typhon.

The *voces magicae* include some of the formulae discussed above. One of the more interesting is the triad of names associated elsewhere in the magical papyri with Hekate: NEBOUTOSOUALÊTH AKTIÔPHI ERESCHIGAL. This formula appears in many places. The last name is that of the Babylonian goddess of the dead, and had begun to appear on Greek curse tablets as early as the fourth century BCE.

"Come to me and go" is a standard formula summoning the god as peer and then instructing him to carry out the operation. "That very person has wronged me and he ... has spilled the blood of Typhon ..." — the slander of the target is more common in Greek love spells generally addressed to Selene. This spell with its Demotic rubrics, Hellenized Babylonian names, and Greek magical method is a good example of the syncretism of late antiquity.

19

The last spell we will examine in this chapter was found during excavations of the Roman wells in Athens. Inscribed in a beautiful scribal hand, it dates from the mid-third century CE. There were several such tablets found bearing variations on this formula. The magician likely possessed a source book from which the spells were copied.

BÔRPHORBABARBORBABARPHORBABORBORBAIÊ, powerful BETPUT I deliver to you Eutuchianos, to whom Eutuchia gave birth, that you may chill him and his resolve, and in your gloomy air also those who are with him. Bind him in the unlit realm of oblivion, chill and destroy the wrestling which he is about to do in the De . . . ei this coming Friday. And if he does wrestle, I hand over to you, MOZOUNÊ ALCHEINÊ PERPERTHARÔNA IAIA, Eutuchianos, to whom Eutuchia gave birth, in order that he may fall down and reveal himself a fool. Powerful Typhon KOLCHOI TONTONON Seth SATHAÔCH EA Lord APOMX PHRIOURIGX, regarding the disappearing and chilling of Eutuchianos, to whom Eutuchia gave birth. KOLCHOICHEILÔPS. Let Eutuchianos grow cold and not be in condition this coming Friday, but let him be weak. As these names grow cold, so let Eutuchianos grow cold, to whom Eutuchia gave birth. whom Aithalês promotes.

"I deliver to you" is a common Greek formula wherein the victim is made the god's property. "Chill him and his resolve" and following references to cold and dark are the especial domains of Set (as early as the Pyramid texts — for example in the spell of obtaining the Tcham scepter — "Giver of Winds). KOLCHOI TONTONON is a secret name of Set-Typhon. APOMX is an alternate spelling of APOMPS appearing above. "As those names grow cold" the physical fate of the tablet in the cold spring water effects the cursed wrestler. Over a hundred tablets were found in this spot alone, a tribute if not to the efficacy of magic, at least to the popular belief in the sorcerer who created them.

The erudition and magical skill of the creators of the papyri and tablets were great. Their intelligence was put to what they considered a powerful and practical endeavor, and knowing the secret that what has worked before can work again, these technologies can be effectively reapplied.

Such an application is not merely the use of practical sorcery. It is the active forging of a Link to the Past and the needs of the

Now. Such magic subtly works on the Memory (*Anamnesis*) and prepares the psyche for revelations which will occur at a later stage of Initiation.

Chapter 3
Set

When you receive a revelation of this one, the one you
must know, for you are ignorant of yourself when you
are ignorant of him, you may be filled with Fear because
of the great dynamism of that place — then you flee
backwards to your body. But if you desire to Become
perfect, you will remain in that place and still
yourself.

Allogenes

The Egyptian god Set went through periods of immense
popularity alternating with total denunciation. Set in the
predynastic and archaic periods was an essentially positive deity
introduced from the east as a god of the *extension of existence*.
He is therefore god of *expanding* borders and radical changes of
being, particularly birth, circumcision/initiation, death in battle,
and rebirth through the Opening of the Mouth ceremony. Popular
among easterners, his first cult site being Pelusium in the eastern
Delta, his worship quickly spread to *border* areas, where he was
identified with local gods of initiation. Two examples of such cult
sites are Kharga in the south, which has always been primarily a
Nilotic culture area, and the Libyan settlement of Ombos, wherein
Set was identified with the local god Ash in the IInd dynasty.
Set's original worship as a nighttime/polar deity suffered a
decline with the rise of solar worship in the IVth dynasty. The
Great Pyramid of Khufu is one of the last early monuments
connected with the idea of a Setian afterlife as well as a solar
one. The Great Pyramid had a special air shaft for the king's *akh*
to fly to the star Alpha Draconis, which is the star of Set in the
Constellation of the Thigh, principle of the Seven Faces of
Darkness.

During the Middle Kingdom, Set was reduced to a symbol of
Upper Egypt and apparently seen only during the Setian festival
of *heb-sed*, or tying together. It was during this time that Set was
first blamed for the murder of Osiris, a Semitic corn god who
had arrived in the IIIrd dynasty. Previously, Osiris had died of
drowning. No matter how "evil" Set was, the essential function of
Set, of going out and expanding the borders of existence and
then returning that Chaotic energy to the center, always
continued. It is the darkness that binds together the Egyptian
light.

The foreigners who ruled Egypt known as the Hyksos —
quite probably Hurrians — actively identified themselves with Set
and established their capital at an ancient Setian site, Avaris.
Very little is known about their religious or magical practices,
although excavations going on at the time of writing this book
should reveal great wealth. But they were great horsemen, and
the horse (like the ass) had became identified with Set. It
required Hyksos rule before, after almost 200 years of its use in
Egypt, that evil Setian animal the horse could be protrayed in
Egyptian art.

The second native blooming of Setian thinking may have
begun in the XVIIIth dynasty, but certainly it reached its peak in
the XIXth and XXth dynasties when a family of Setian priests
from Tanis became the pharaonic line. During this time of
expanding borders, Set was extraordinarily popular, as can be
seen from pharaohs' names such as Seti (Set's man) and Setnakt
(Set is Mighty). Two important Setian texts were produced: First,
the "Tale of Two Brothers," which tells how Set (identified with
the god Bata) undergoes a series of metamorphoses ($\chi eperu$) that
change him from a farm hand to a star in the Constellation of
the Thigh. The second text is the *Book of Knowing the Spiral
Force of Re and the Felling of Apep*. This protective formula,
which Ramses III, son of Setnakt, inscribed on certain border
monuments, shows two Setian particularities. Firstly, it has an
unnamed god coming into being in the psychic (subjective) realm
as the god $\chi ephra$ — previously it had been held that Neith, a
goddess of nature, had transformed herself into the $\chi ephra$ beetle.
Secondly, the spell gives the magician one of the powers of Set,
which is to slay Apep, the dragon of delusion.

With the coming of the XXIInd dynasty, Egypt entered its
long decline. Set became a tremendously unpopular deity. His
worship ceased everywhere except the oases and the city of
Thebes, where his cult was absorbed into the cult of Montu, the
warlord of Thebes. The negative and destructive aspects of
isolation and destruction were emphasized and as Egypt turned
more to an idealized past, Set-Heh, the god of the void called the
future, came to resemble the Christian Satan.

The third blooming came with the coming of the Greeks to
Egypt. It is from this period that the Hellenic notions of
independence and self-worth began to revive both the operant
and initiatory aspects of the New Kingdom Set cult. The spells in
this volume are taken in the main from the third blooming. The
success of Graeco-Egyptian magic, despite Roman persecution, saw
an expansion of both the philosophical and magical aspects of this

24

tradition as far north as Britain. The third century of the Common Era was the height of Setian Hermeticism. For useful magical and cultural background on that time of super-individuation, see especially *Spiritual Guides of the Third Century* by Richard Valantasis. With the coming of Christianity as a state religion, individualism was again despised. The Coptic fathers identified Set with Satan, and he almost disappears as a figure in Egyptian magic. The European manuals gave way to medieval grimoires and perhaps the last practicing Setian, the 8th century Abulfaiz Dhu'l Nun, changed his name to Thuban the Black (Thuban being the name of the star Alpha Draconis). Thuban as Pir, or Chief of his Order, was called "King or Lord of the Fish" (the fish being a Typhonic animal). Thuban was third in teaching succession after Daud of Tai and Maaruf Karkhi (in the Order of the Builders). Thuban founded the Malamti, or "blameworthy," order of Sufi, which has certain similarities with Freemasonry. The Masonic Pillar of the Temple "Boaz" (the black pillar) may be "Albuazz," a form of Thuban's name Abulfaiz.

The fourth blooming began in the middle of the nineteenth century, when Western occultism began to focus seriously on archaeological data coming from Egypt. Particularly important highlights were

• The publication of the Rite of the Headless One, in which the deity the magician *transforms himself into* has certain Typhonic names.

• Aleister Crowley's success with that invocation in April 8, 9, and 10 of 1904, wherein part of his revelation consisted of the audible word Coph(rr) — which is the Word of Set.

• April 30, 1966, when Anton Szandor LaVey founded the Church of Satan and began a magical exploration of the psychological factors of the Christian Satan.

• 1972, when Anton LaVey published *The Satanic Rituals*, which included *die elektrischen Vorspiele*, which was privately known as the Rite of the Is-To-Be. This text, based on the Eighth Precept of the Emerald Tablet of Hermes

Use your mind to its full extent and rise from Earth to Heaven, and then again descend to Earth and combine the powers of what is above and what is below. Thus you will win glory in the whole world, and obscurity will leave you at once.

This is largely an invocation to Anubis, Opener of the Way, to cause power to flow forth under the control of the Children of Set (so named).

25

• North Solstice, 1975, Michael A. Aquino invoked Set and receives the *Book of Coming Forth by Night*. Empowered by this gnosis, Aquino becomes a Magus and founds the Temple of Set, which has a similar appeal to postmodern magicians that Set-Typhon did in Late Antiquity. Once again Set, whose name means "Initiation", is highly honored upon this Earth.

• September 9, 1995, under the guidance of the researchers of the Order of Setne Khamuast, the Temple of Set has a *heb-sed* festival at the oasis of Las Vegas.

The serious postmodern magician seeks out scholarly data for the same reason his counterpart in Egypt did, precision. In order to Open the Mouth of the Gods, which is the essentially Setian act, one must have as precise a contact with the entities as possible.

The name and image of Set are among the scholarly problems of Egyptology. Set's appearance and disappearance from the pantheon is not discussed. The former concerns can provide the magician with some useful data, the latter is tied up with the esoteric nature of Set and becomes a key in understanding the god, which is the first step in assuming the Form of the god to work your will upon the universe.

Set, in the papyri (Σηθ), evolved from Sūt to Sēt. The meaning of the name is unclear — various pseudo-etymologies belonging to the Egyptians show some of the thought processes concerned with the word. Plutarch, who translated it as the "Overpowering One," captured the general understanding of Set-Typhon as a Fate-like force of compulsion — and it is in this Form that the name of Set exists in the papyri. The magician having Worked his or her will in the state of having reached Set (PAKERBÊTH), made his will into a predetermined Fate. "Set" came almost to mean "Anankê" — and indeed since that goddess was associated with the Pole Star, both were seen as rulers over the rotating stars, which in turn ruled Fate.

The most likely root of the name "Set" is a word meaning Isolator or Elector. Some of the earliest hieroglyphs of Set are written with the knife (⚒), which was presumed to be a castration tool, but recent work by Roth suggests might be the birthing knife (or *Pesh-Khent*). The birthing knife, which was later associated with the goddesses Renet and Meskhent, is a symbol of destiny, birth, and re-birth.

Set is generally portrayed as a fantastic animal; however, there are certain animals associated with him. These are the ass, the horse, the giraffe, the hippopotamus, the crocodile, the black boar — particularly in its form of *sab*, the "destiny beast" — and the leopard of the south. Set is portrayed as a reclining beast with a fantastic head featuring a long snoot and square-tipped, brush-like ears. His tail is forked in the shape of the birthing knife. Alternately, he's portrayed as a man with the beast's head. Rarer representations include a winged minotaur, a bull-headed serpent, and simply a man in foreign dress. In late antique times he was portrayed as an ass-headed man, and as representations of him were made further and further away from Egypt, this form predominated. Although the Egyptians portrayed *aku* demons as fabulous beasts, Set alone of the gods was portrayed as a fabulous animal — perhaps signifying his separation from the natural order. He is likely the same god as the Sumerian griffin — which ended up as the Peacock Melek T'aus or the god Rudra.

In the classical period Set's weapon was generally a spear topped by a birthing knife. He used this to slay the serpent Apep, much as the midwife cut the umbilical cord. This action nightly freed the barque of Re to continue its journey. Notably this battle occurs in the early morning, a time when many people are having to cut through the tenacious strands of what has not come into being and re-establish themselves as an individual. Other items carried by Set are a *waz* or *tcham* (pronounced "djam") scepter — a stylized representation of himself ( ). Many gods carried these symbols. *Waz* signifies power in this world, *tcham* signifies power especially through one's progeny or an army. In Late Antiquity (particularly on curse tablets found outside of Egypt), Set carries a flail — presumably to punish lesser gods and demons and to compel them to perform his will.

In classical times Set was painted red or gold depending on his status in society. Red is the Egyptian color of evil, associated with the hostile forces of the desert, the "Red Land." The papyri of Thebes separate "good" operations (those that integrate the magician with the eternal patterns of Nature), which required lamps of any color but red, and "evil" operations (those that sought to impose the magician's will either on the non-ego parts of himself or upon the world), which required red lamps. In fact, the requirement of a red lamp is an encoded indication of a Setian/Typhonic spell. During the Setian dynasties (XIX-XX) Set enjoyed the same gold flesh as the other gods. Set was occasionally portrayed as black because of his connection with the night sky; as Mediterranean ideas of the "color" of evil began to affect Egypt, Set became black. In our own cultural milieu, black rather than red will perhaps work better for the magician seeking to emulate Set.

27

The dwelling place of Set is an interesting question. Most Egyptian gods dwell in three realms — on this Earth, where an "image" of them may be seen, like Re; in the Duat, the Egyptian underworld where they often have a mummiform appearance like Ptah; or hidden in the sky, perhaps as a star or in the Island of Fire. The last is sometimes the dwelling place of the gods — but more often their place of origin. The god χephra was born there, and the Island of Fire is perhaps a symbol of the burning mind of man which produces gods. Although Set can be in these places (including mummiform Set statues), he is generally conceived of as being behind or beyond the celestial dome. Specifically, he is behind the Constellation of the Thigh. These are the seven stars we refer to as the Big Dipper, and may be viewed as a Sign of Set's manifestation in the objective universe.

These Seven Stars were known to the Egyptians as the Imperishable Stars. So called because they do not set but revolve counterclockwise during the whole of the night. The earliest funerary cult (Ist-IIIrd dynasties) of the Egyptians was a stellar cult, wherein the dead would rise to the sky and become a star; these stars became a symbol of immortality. This period was marked by boat burials where the prow of the boat pointed North toward the undying stars. During the XIXth and XXth dynasties, the Setian pharaohs revived this symbology (note the "Tale of Two Brothers" above). When Babylonian ideas of astrology were introduced to Egypt, the seven stars became symbols of Fate. After all, if the stars of the Zodiac which rose and fell — appeared and disappeared at certain seasons — ruled action on this world, surely the stars they revolved around must be the most potent rulers!

Greek thinking, also influenced by the Persians, gave the polar stars a special place as well. They were seen as the top of Fate's spindle (note Plato's analogy of the Spindle of Necessity in the *Republic*). Set came to be seen as the Secret (i.e., known only to the magician) Ruler of the Cosmos.

I would like to examine what is mythologically known from classical Egyptian sources concerning Set's activity in each of the three worlds — the Duat, the Earth, and the Celestial region — and look at the Sethos, or Secret Region, which appears in the gnostic religious literature of Late Antiquity. If the magicians who seek to transform themselves into Set know what (and where) Set performs, they can perform these same actions with greater precision. Thus Set is both a role model for initiation and a source of patterns-of-consciousness for operative magic.

28

Set in the Duat. Set's appearance in the Duat is twofold. He is either a punisher of the wicked or the savior of Re.

In the first role, he is the Ruler of the first section of the Duat — Set-Amentet. This region is conceived of in space as the area beneath the sunset, in time as the first hour of darkness, or symbolically the time immediately after the *ka* and the *ba* of the deceased have removed themselves from the body and gone wandering. This also gives Set authority over out-of-the-body states and his traditional role as sender of nightmares. These frightening images are to be understood by the magician as testers, manifestations of Set's role as demonic initiator. They can likewise be used as weapons *by* the magician.

In his role as tormenter of the wicked, Set appears in various guises in the Duat. He is the heart-eating dragon SetNakt (Set is Mighty). SetNakt eats the *heart* (intellect) of the evil individual. He is the figure of Set the Watcher, who observes the progress of the Boat of Re. This role is one of observer of the Real, a role that he also fills in slaying the demon Apep. Nightly the Boat of Re is challenged by the *non-created* serpent Apep. Apep has the power to hypnotize the other inhabitants of the boat. The other gods fall into a trance, the Boat stops, and Set descends to fight the demon. He kills Apep with a spear topped with a Pesh-Khent knife. The Pesh-Khent knife is used both by midwives to sever umbilical cords and by *sem* priests to perform the Opening of the Mouth ceremony. The forked knife (Υ) is an image of Set's tail.

These roles may be seen as the same. Set is a destroyer of delusional thinking. He destroys that which has failed to Become real. As such he is a tester of the dead — a god of Limits. In short, Set works in the subconscious as a destroyer of delusion.

Set on Earth. Set is the god of the desert, of foreign lands. He was highly honored by the Pharaohs of the Empire period (XIXth and XXth dynasties). As a god of foreign lands, he was easily identified with nearby storm and desert gods — Ash of the Libyans, Teshub of the Hittites, Baal of the Syrians, Tishpak of the Hurrians, Ninazu of the Ubaidians, and even with YHWH of the Hebrews.

His primary cult sites such as Ombos and Tanis were neglected (or even destroyed) after the rise of Osiris, god of stasis, in the XXIth dynasty. But the outlying shrines — the shrines at the oases such as Kharga and Dahlke — remained active even into Roman times. It is from these centers that the archetype of Set returned to Egypt in late antique times.

Set's presence on Earth was primarily as a *change* agent. As such, he was the god of χ*eper* or development, versus *Wen* or stasis. He was invoked in the Empire period (the XVIIIth-XXth dynasties) as a healer in his *green deeds*. Spells and charms abounded against him as storm god, causer of abortions, and sender of nightmares.

Just as Set is an ender of delusional thought in the Duat, he is a *sender* of delusional thought on Earth. His ability to send dreams and nightmares has always been sought by the magician. In magical operations, he is primarily an agent of *psychic disruption* or a sender of confusion.

In this role he "shakes up" the minds of others the magician wishes to influence. This is the second part of Setian magic. In the Duat, Set limits the manifestation of unreal thoughts of the magician. The now habitually clear-headed Setian uses the same disruptive power upon *the earth* — upon others so that he or she may broadcast his or her thoughts into the minds of others. This relationship is shown in the names and titles of a XXth dynasty pharaoh, Setnakt. His name Setnakt means Set-Is-Mighty — the identical name of one of the testers in the Duat. His grandson Ramses IV recorded that Setnakt was "like χeper-i-Set in his rage" upon the battlefield. By using the power of Set — the battlefield-might — he was able to create a space in which development might occur.

The role of Set upon this world is to clear a space wherein an individually determined creation may occur.

Set in the Celestial Region. Set's interaction with the gods is (like Typhon's) a primarily hostile one. He is the slayer of Osiris and usually the enemy of his brother Horus.

The slaying of Osiris, which probably was originally the slaying of Sokaris — Osiris having come to Egypt in historic time — is the great blow against stasis. The Egyptians conceived of two types of time, *Neheh* and *djet*. *Neheh* was the eternal future. It was conceived of as a great spiral uncoiling into the now. The events of the future tended to pass by one's eyes again and again — growing clearer with each revolution until they finally came into being. *Djet* was the linear past. It was unchanging, stretching back from the now an infinite distance. It was ruled by Osiris. It held all that has happened as well as the "images" rather than the true form of the gods. As such it contains all of the common material in all subjective universes as well as all observable things in the objective universe. Set is ever in opposition to the god Osiris; his slaying of Osiris is an ongoing process and is felt by mankind by any form of longing they experience.

When a person wants anything, a *ka* or image of that desire appears in the *Neheh* or future. This is a region ruled by Set under his cult title of Set-Heh. The desire pulls that person toward the event and sets him in opposition with the matrix of the past, or *djet*. If he or she succeeds in obtaining (making real) the desire, he or she has slain Osiris. However, the new object immediately becomes part of the matrix of the past.

In the magical papyri the great matrix of the past is called the "hollow of Osiris the Beautiful." The bringing of new things into that matrix is symbolized by the judgment the gods visit upon Set — making him tote around the mummiform corpse of Osiris on his back in the form of Bata, the ever-χepering Bull of Ombos. This interaction between cultural conservatism (Osiris) and Set's Remanifestations provides the postmodern (or "Aeonic Age") magician certain clues about the "pulse" of history.

Set's role as god of the future places him in opposition to the other gods, whose role is that of maintainers of cosmic order.

Set's other celestial role, that of the enemy and/or friend of the Great Horus, is a bit more complex. The Great Horus, god of sunlight, represents an ordered (perhaps even harmonious) response to chaos. He represents the *vital* active part of the seen world. His visible manifestation is the pharaoh, the incarnation of the *idea* of mankind. The flying falcon, his mode is visual. He is engaged in a constant fight with his brother Set. In this fight, Set plucks out Horus' right eye, and Horus pulls away Set's testicles. Later the two combatants are gathered at the city of Hermopolis by Toth, god of the moon, and reconciled. Set regains his testicles and Horus his eye. The theft of seed is the passing of the *Tcham* power into the visible world. It is the source of the attraction between the teacher (the human mediator of Initiation) and student. The powerful attraction — this idea of Beauty — can lead to serious abuses and confusions. The theft of the Eye is the absorption of knowledge into Set's realm where it returns as energized world plans.

Unlike the simple myth of Set and Osiris where the influence of a dead monarch is made holy and powerful, the interaction of Set and Horus is a myth of conflict (of *hnnw*, storm) between the visible present and the individualist. Notably at times such as the Heb-Sed festival the two warring gods become the "Two Partners."

Whereas Osiris is the god of the deified or efficacious past (*djet*), both Set and Horus are gods of the magical future (*neheh*). In the Old Kingdom, a special game symbolized their interaction, called *Mehen*.

31

The *Mehen* game was a spiral game board shaped after and named after an underworld serpent, *Mehen*. The two players raced with marbles and lion figures into a central area — the region of Re. Re is equated with the ultimately Real — to see Re was not to merge with this reality, but to have the strength of being to be able to see the real — to bypass all that has failed to come into being. That the entrance to the realm is by means of a *struggle* (a *hnnw*) between the forces of individualism and cooperation reveals the two paths to the divine — which span Egyptian history as *sem-neter* (servant of the gods) and *paχer-neter* (reaching the level of the gods).

By the time of the New Kingdom, the rules to the *Mehen* game had been forgotten, but the symbol of the game — a spiral in which Horus and Set are united — remained. Two Coffin Text spells (493 and 495) mention the mysteries of *Mehen* (*shtau Mehen*):

"My *ba* belongs to its body; my shadow belongs to its condition. I am the guard of criminals in the manner of the mysteries of *Mehen*."

This reference to secret knowledge of mysteries connected with the figure that unites Horus and Set bespeaks of the special magical relationship between Horus-Set and the future. This secret knowledge is private information concerning the interior life which can only be passed from teacher to student. It is more than mere words and partakes of both social mysteries and magic in the strictest sense. *Mehen* is ultimately the coils of the *future* Horus and Set, two principles of consciousness that both in contention and cooperation cause the efficacious future to manifest on this earth. The ultimate example of the *Mehen* mystery is found in a funerary text of the New Kingdom called the *Book of Pylons*. In this book Re, representing the deceased, travels through a series of gateways in the Duat. In each he is menaced ultimately by the Apep serpent, the god of that which has not come into being. When this creature is slain by Set, Re emerges into the Tenth Hour, otherwise known as the kingdom of χephra. One of the beings aiding him into this transition is a remarkable figure called "His Two Faces."

This shows a creature bearing the heads of Horus and Set. This figure, which accompanies the sun god during his regeneration into Xephra, the Self-Created One, is *Mehen*.

> *Mehen WP n iarw.t khensof dwa.t*
> *Smrw.t rmn.Sn khwy.f(y) m shta.f*
> It is *Mehen* of the Uraei, he travels through the Duat.
> The bows, they lift up His Two Faces in the form of the Mystery.

The relationship of Horus and Set symbolizes the struggle between individuality and cooperation. Yet from time to time that struggle comes into a place of unity which is an essentially protective and regenerative function.

Notably the last appearance of the name of Horus-Set is in a general spell for obtaining favor, honor and passion in the Coptic tongue — where Horus-Set is invoked among a list of angels such as Michael and Gabriel (London Hay 10434). This appearance of Horus-Set in the seventh century of the common era is the last known until the twentieth century.

Beyond the celestial manifestations of Set, there are references to a fourth or "secret" region. In the earliest times this was a place for those who died in battle; the gateway or Mouth (Re) to this place was ruled by the psychopompic god of the battlefield dead — in Upper Egypt, Sokaris and in Lower Egypt, Anubis. This region of mysterious pathways was called *Setaue* and was originally conceived of as being behind the seven stars we call the Big Dipper.

Set was conceived of as the slayer of the royal dead. He killed the pharaoh — afterall the pharaoh could not fall at the hands of mortals.

When the Osirian and solar funerary cults came to power the special "mysterious place" either vanished (or merely became part of the Duat).

The idea of a special region ruled by Set returned at various times. It enjoyed popularity during the XIXth and XXth dynasties when the night sky was portrayed in royal tombs. Notably in the royal burials at Tanis, where the families of the Setian pharaohs of the XIXth and XXth dynasties were buried, the sarcophagi were made in the form of Sokaris rather than Osiris. Sokaris, as Lord of the Mouth of the Passages of the Secret Place, might be said to *be* the lord of the seven stars of the Big Dipper. In an esoteric sense this may indicate that Fear is the mother of Initiation — or more properly that the overcoming of Fear is the beginning of Self-development. Sokaris, in his role of god of the battlefield, is the god who represents all of the complexity of courage and fear — of death in the service of the Living Horus. Since these interactions produce the wealth of the psyche, Sokaris was early on identified with Ptah. Only later did identification with Osiris occur.

Sokaris had as his consort Sekhmet. This name is merely the feminine form of the word for divine power (Sekhem). This refers to the power that comes from facing fear. Soldiers wore red rings indicating that in their next life they would enjoy sexual relations with Sekhmet. That power was seen as sexually desirable and available only after facing great fear is at the heart of the Hermetic tradition, and has undergone a remanifestation in the antinomian aspect of the current Setian revival.

Beyond Sokaris and Sekhmet, beyond Struggle and Beauty, is the secret place of Set. To venture into this place is to Become the source of the future, to become the Ruler of the rulers of Fate.

It is the ultimate goal of the Hermetic tradition, and is the Setian way.

Chapter 4
Theory

Blessed is the man who knows these things, who has
brought Heaven down upon Earth and has taken Earth and
lifted it up unto Heaven, and has created thereby a Void
for himself.

The Book of the Gnosis
of the Invisible God

I. The Historical Matrix

In the XXVIth dynasty, Egyptian pharaohs hired Greek
mercenaries and the resultant cultural exchange produced the
Hermetic tradition, a synthesis of Egyptian magical cosmology and
Greek philosophical speculation. The cosmological background was
established by the time of the death of Alexander and reached its
individualist height 600 years later. I will examine the Greek and
Egyptian contributions to the Hermetic world view and then
present a synthetic account of Hermetic theory as it applies to the
Setian-Typhonic practitioner of today.

Egypt provided two ideas to the Hermetic mixture. The first
is the belief in the strength of the idea, and the second is the
notion of the cycles of creation which culminate in self-creation.
The invasion of foreigners provided the idea that magic might be
applied to individual efforts rather than for supporting the cosmic
order. Each of these ideas deserves to be examined.

II. The Power of the Idea

The Two Lands came into being as an idea. Some time
around 3100 BCE Narmer, the first pharaoh, united his Southern
culture (African) with that of the North (Asian/Semitic). Two
peoples racially and linguistically separate were tied together
through magical ceremonies that insisted they were now a unity.
The strength of Narmer's politico-magical working is seen not
only in that Egypt lasted for 3000 years, but that as a magical
concept Egypt still draws the mind as no other. Consider how
many magical and religious organizations both in antiquity and
today claim roots from Narmer's working — from the *idea* of
Egypt.

During the times of kingdom and empire, the *idea* of Egypt
was incarnated in the pharaoh. The idea was strong enough to
preserve and enhance the culture even when the pharaohs were
not Egyptian by birth. The Grecian Ptolemies were accepted by
the Egyptians because they made the ritual gestures, adopted the

magical titles. The Persians, who made little or no attempt at connecting with the *idea* of Egypt, were despised. The fanaticism that causes an idea to be incarnated is Egypt's legacy to the world.

Most Egyptian non-medical magic was of two sorts — sending emotions or ideas into others, or receiving emotions or ideas from a divine source. Spells to send madness (*Neba*), melancholy (*dehkert*), or "evil sleep" abound — whereas sendings for death are rare. Magic (*heka*) also is derived from having insight (*sia*). Understanding the world was the greatest key to magic and therefore the primary goal of the magician was the seeking out of creative Understanding. Creative Understanding was a fusion of the two perceptive facilities of intellect and emotion and of the hidden god of the psyche (see Chapter 7 on the uniting of Shu, Tefnut, and the Unnamed God). Magical power may be gained by an astral journey to the Island of Fire (*Aa-nsernser-t*) the birthplace of the god χephra where magical power is generated against the forces of Chaos (Apep) counteracting the renewal of cosmic life. It can likewise be gained by journeys to places of a transitional nature, such as the horizon. This idea became the notion for both Gnostic and Hermetic ascents. Likewise, magical power could be taught (*sba*) by "savior" gods or by living humans.

If the idea is used to steer a group wherein one man or woman thinks the idea and all embody it as a group — then it will lead inevitably to totalitarianism and loss of human dignity. If the idea is embodied in unique individuals rather than a group, it can lead to a personal empowerment that comes as close to godhood as can be obtained under the fetters of life and nature. This *use* of an idea alone lasted long after the decline of Hermetic thinking in Egypt and was one of the first notions of Hermeticism to be revived in Europe during the Renaissance. Among its remanifestations are the American Revolution. The power of the idea has predictably come to the individual level again; however, unlike its previous manifestation in a limited geographic and social milieu — it now is available on a global scale.

However, it is a hard path and few will dare it.

III. The Cycles of Creation

A particularly Egyptian idea is that Creation is becoming further defined against a matrix of chaos *and* knowing the path of definition becomes a source of power. Many Mediterranean cultures emphasize the evolutionary nature of creation. Matter is created by the oldest gods who through reproductive acts create those gods who change what is already created and conditioned. The Egyptian magician took this formula a step further. He would become the next god in line to have a hand at modifying creation. As such he would have to first modify his *own* creation, he would have to become self-created.

This apparent paradox is at the heart of Egyptian religious hymns. The hymn may begin by describing the origin of the Cosmos speaking of the acts of some creator god such as Atum (whose name means simultaneously "He who is perfect" and "He who does not exist") and the successive generation of gods until the god to whom the hymn was written, say the craftsman Ptah, is mentioned. The object of adoration is then declared "He who is created of himself." χefer - des.f This expression appears at least as early as the Pyramid Texts of the Old Kingdom (and perhaps earlier since the hieroglyph for χephra, the rising sun whose name is derived from the root that means "being and becoming," appears among the first writing in predynastic sites). This Ramesside idea passed into the Graeco-Egyptian synthesis a year after the conquest of Egypt by Alexander: the Bremner-Rhind papyrus was written. One of the spells for slaying Apep begins as a cosmogony in which the Lord of Differentiated Existence begins merely by describing the process of his coming into being with the words χepra χeper χeperu. The highest magic was essentially a narration that establishes the speaker as ultimate subject and the universe as object. However, the process of knowing the past and then separating oneself from it in order to enact a new creation is an essential act of Hermetic practice. (See Chapter 7 on the Bremner-Rhind papyrus and its significance.)

The doctrine of the Logos (Λογος), which came to encode the cycles of creation, filled Gnostic and Hermetic thought. Of particular interest is the *Codex Brucianus*, a Coptic text written in the third century that describes the powers of Words to Create Aeons, which may be viewed as ladder rungs to the divine. The supreme Aeon is that of the Alone-begotten one (αυτογενης). To this Aeon all move through their actions, by changing the Aeons beneath. This path of power through magical control is the essential Setian goal.

Portions of the *Codex Brucianus* were published by Golden Dawn member Florence Farr and were adapted by Aleister Crowley into his theories of Magi, Words, and Aeons. These Egyptian ideas of the cycles of creation pervade and structure most Western magic. The remanifestation of these ideas allow the current magician to make even more powerful use of them than his counterpart of late antiquity.

IV. The Idea of Individualism

Individualism as a virtue was a notion alien to Egypt (and therefore its arrival was first identified with Set, god of foreigners). The Egyptian cosmology also had a primary focus on the pharaoh, who as the Living Horus was an *incarnation of the idea of mankind*. Early funerary cults were based entirely on this figure who was the mediator between gods, men, and the dead. One's relationship to the universe depended on one's relationship to the pharaoh.

Only in the XVIIIth dynasty does a word signifying an individual appear. Popular funerary cults focused on the idea of identification of the dead with Osiris.

The individualist had been tarred by the label "Setian" as early as the *Dream Book* (a text written in the Middle Kingdom but our only copy is from the XIXth dynasty).

> The god in him is Seth ... he is a man of the people —
> He dies by a death of ... the fallings ... sinews ... He is
> one dissolute of heart on the day of judgment ...
> discontent in his heart. If he drinks beer, he drinks it to
> engender strife and turmoil. The redness of the white of
> his eye is this god. He is one who drinks what he
> detests. He is beloved of women through the greatness —
> the greatness of his loving them. Though he is a royal
> kinsman, he has the personality of a man of the people ...
> He will not descend unto the west, but is placed on the
> desert as a prey to rapacious birds ... He drinks beer so
> as to engender turmoil and disputes ... He will take up
> weapons of warfare — He will not distinguish the
> married woman from ... As to any man who opposes him
> he pushes ... Massacre arises in him and he is placed in
> the Netherworld....

But only with the coming of the Greeks did the notion of individualism as a good appear in Egyptian thinking. Perhaps the spirit of magic (my will be done) was on par with — or superior to — the spirit of religion (thy will be done).

V. Magical Control

There is a two-fold division in Hermetic magic, operant magic to get one's needs, and initiatory magic to learn what one truly needs. The spells in this book are predominantly of the first sort — operations for love, protection, and blessing the workplace. The nature of this work is clear to anyone.

The other type of magic can be termed illustrative or initiatory. These magical formulae deal with enacting the lifetime process of Initiation. They are like the rites of passage performed by religionists, but they are separated from these by an important factor — they represent an individual rather than a social change. Rites of passage inform and integrate an individual into society. For example, a rite communicating passage into adulthood informs the society that the individual involved is now possessed of certain responsibilities and powers. An initiatory rite informs the *psyche* of the individual that he or she is now possessed of certain powers and responsibilities. Initiatory magic — when practiced by the individual — separates him- or herself from the social matrix.

Initiation does not occur *within* the magical chamber, but it is illustrated there. One does not enter into adulthood by (say) receiving one's high school diploma, but that action illustrates a variety of other processes which may have occurred. It's easy for the high school graduate to know that *something* has happened, the ritual being boosted by not only his cap and gown, but those of his peers, the music, the crowds, etc. The magician has ultimately only his or her will to provide the knowledge of the change. *In short, to work magic that changes the self, the magician's will must be as strong in his or her subjective universe as the massed wills of others appear to be.* Once this strength of will is obtained, magical control of one's life follows. As long as an individual is more strongly motivated by shame or fear or the desire for acceptance, he or she cannot practice magic of an initiatory nature. The figure of Set-Typhon, rebel against the gods, can not be invoked in a psyche motivated by external stimuli.

To the extent that the magician successfully becomes as Set-Typhon in an operation — the operation has an initiatory and/or illustrative component. One does not merely become divine to take on the power of a god, but to take on the wisdom of the god. As magicians increase in their power, the rites practiced will become more free of preprogrammed ritual. The words of power, the *voces magicae* will become more and more precise tools used to gain *access* to divine states. The magician will (after practice) free him- or herself from the texts, and as each *successful* immortalization of the soul occurs, the magician begins to act on a more and more divine level. For the advanced magician every act becomes a magical one. He or she is said to have become magic (*heka*) itself.

Most who aspire to this divine state fail in one of two ways. The first (and most common) is to assume that they have reached this state because they can comprehend it. Surely, they reason, if I know this thing I am this thing. This is also why many people who have never tried their hand at filling a single blank page believe that they can write the Great American Novel. The magician should set ever-greater tasks for him- or herself — greater feats of magic to perform. The Setian magician should avoid that sense of stasis (*wen*) that characterizes Osiris but seek that state of embracing constant growth (*χeper*) that characterizes Set (and allows him to rise above Order and Chaos). The second form of failure is to seek power without acknowledging that all parts of the body-soul complex are thusly empowered. Many magicians who achieve that great wonder of wisdom, fail to note that without its daily use, the great monsters of the id are quite ready to exert control. The phenomenon of life keeps us full of ill-will and desires that do naught but hinder us if we give them unthinking power.

Such empowerment may not only make us petty tyrants but has a long-term spiritual effect as well. The state of becoming an effective spirit (an *akh*), which is the goal of the Typhonian Hermeticist, is not a sure one. One may very well become a vengeful spirit (a *mut*), whose limited function is to punish the living. The *akh* continues to influence life on this Earth in order to shape a place that it may remanifest for future revelation. The *mut* merely tortures those whom it hates. The *mut* may be invoked by the magician for his dirty work. There are many of them, for the world is filled with great hatred.

If one cannot bring about events by will alone during one's lifetime, when one is most closely linked to this world, one will definitely not be able to do so after death. The practice of magical control of one's life is the essential purpose of anyone seeking personal immortality. It constitutes the goal of *Paχer-Netery* and is the hidden meaning of the most powerful of Set-Typhon's names, *PAKERBÊTH* (I have risen to the level of Set).

Chapter 5
Practice

The doors are open for thee in secret places. Stand up,
remove thy earth, shake off thy dust, raise thyself up,
voyage thou with effective spirits. Thy wings are those of
a falcon, thy brightness is that of a star.

Pyramid Texts,
Utterance 419

The core concept of Setian thought is one of *isolation*. This led
to the easy adoption of Set, the isolator, and Typhon, the rebel,
into Hermetic thought, which was keyed to the primacy of the
Mind. The Setian experience is twofold: firstly, of a desire to
change that which exists in the created and conditioned world
that stands forth in the light; and secondly, a desire to expand
into that region of internal and external darkness where growth
is possible.

This is ultimately a guide not only for your use of the spells
in this papyrus, and even for the creation of your own, but for a
Typhonian initiation as well because the two-fold desire reflects a
desire to *change* those aspects of the personality that seem to
have been put in place by the forces of the world, and to *expand*
into those places where the laws are not yet fixed. This quality
which is inherent in the god needs to be inherent in those who
become the god for the purpose of spell-casting. Spells are the
chief weapon in the initiate's fight against the forces of
naturalization. One possessed of a Setian psychological make-up
need not look for opportunities to cast the spells — the life led in
opposition to the structure of the world — the life that brings the
Mind to the fore — will create opportunities for their use.

Some preliminary observations concerning the practice of
magic should be made here. The universe is seen as a complex
of forces some belonging to the natural and some to the spiritual
(or non-natural) realm. The forces which *sustain* visible
appearance are the *kaw* (plural of *ka*). These forces are like the
Forms (ειδη). They have a shape and a power (*sekhem*) to
produce that shape in the manifest world. These sustaining forces
are the products of the gods (*neteru*), living men and women
who use magic (*heka*) and the effective dead (*akhu*). These forces
tend to blend into a ruling unity (*Ma'at*) that reflects the Sense of
Beauty of the Creator. Beyond the realm of existence is a Chaos

41

of unmanifested unordered forms. This chaotic realm always presses close, but is repelled nightly when Set slays the god of divine mindlessness, Apep.

The Setian magician rejects the extremes of Order (*Ma'at*) and its consequent stasis Chaos (*Isfet*) as both prevent his or her self-development in the twofold quest written of above. Therefore, he or she does not attempt to draw on these existing forces, but rather creates with the Mind those *kaw* which will sustain new states of being in the world. These creations will appear at first to be of Darkness and will frighten anyone who is incapable of appreciating the New; with time they will become part of the Order, which will itself prod the Setian nature to act again.

In terms of the visible world, Setian magicians use magic to gain those things they need. But as the physical manifestation appears, the states of being it *brings with it* prompt the Setian to Work again because the new state of being requires new manifestations. Those things brought through the art of magic are *destabilizing*. One can never solve one's problems through magic — one can only create new platforms from which growth will be *required*. This great danger of the art of magic was well known to the authors of the magical papyri. It is a *secret* well hidden by the current merchandising of the occult.

The remarks about items which will manifest in the visible realm goes doubly so for the invisible realm. Any work to obtain communication with the psyche — dream oracles and so forth — will produce very destabilizing results. The information so obtained will live in both the *ba* (the physical and spiritual part of self-continuity) and the Shadow (the part which moves the body and likewise begets children). Seeking the advice of the gods is fatal if one intends to disregard it.

The practice of Setian magic recapitulates the Rite of Opening the Mouth. The magician begins as Osiris, a being tied to the cycles of nature. When magicians cast their first effective spells, the manifestations of the spells "kill" them to the natural order. They now Know that they are capable of actions beyond the realm of the three dimensions and five physical senses. This knowledge, coupled with the spell, place them in a place of liminality — the Pool of Transformations (just as the deceased's *ba* had wandered to the Pool of χephra). The will returns the magician to the real world (just as the *sem* priest coaxed back the *ba* of the deceased). Then the Mouth is Opened and the magician with the knowledge of the existence of a realm beyond the normal is empowered by that Knowledge of that Unknown realm. Knowing this Unknown is the key to the Hermetic Prayer of

Thanksgiving in which the magician thanks the god for having allowed him to act as a god before death. Knowing the Unknown of the self is an operative key to magic. The phrase "Know Thyself" does appear in the magical papyri, not as an empty philosophical truism but as a key to the door of magic.

The practice of magic will then lead you through transformative times. You will be as Osiris, slain (and resurrected) by Set. You will paradoxically also be Set acting as your own initiator in the role of the Isolator.

The physical requirements for the practice of magic of the Typhonian Hermetic are those items needed to bind the will of the magician on earth. This binding will be of three kinds. Firstly, long term — binding those elements which by owning and using them reflect a commitment of the magician to the process of immortalization of the soul through magic. Secondly, those elements which permit the short-term binding of the magician's will to a given instance to magic. Thirdly, the elements which sustain the magician in his body in such a way as to attune his body-soul complex to his long-term goal of gaining magical power (*heka*). I'll discuss each of these classes of items.

Items of long-term commitment. You will need the following:

• An altar at which you may stand or be seated at a comfortable height to *write* your papyrus. The altar should have four clean bricks on it when work is performed. The bricks, typically arranged in a single layer, represent the primal Earth mound. Moving items onto or off the bricks is putting things into or out of the world. The bricks need not be present during the writing of a spell.

• A symbol of Set-Typhon. This should be chosen according to your taste. It can be an idol or something as simple as an iron sheet with the word ΣΗΘ painted on it in red. This item must be concealed from profane eyes after you have worked with it. This "hiding" has the twofold effect of connecting your practice with that of Egyptian temples, whose inner sancta were never seen; and secondly and more importantly causing the idea of the god to sink into you, when you are about your mundane life.

• A lamp which emits a red light. The author uses a small oil lamp shaped like a volcano, whose reddened glass is colored by the ash of Mt. St. Helens. Red is the color associated with Set-Typhon — and Set-Typhon's influence could be banished with non-red lamps. The Typhonian Hermeticist is free to use red in all of his or her magical operations.

• A robe of dark red or black. Special garments are not required by the tradition — but they are helpful in creating the sense of *isolation* from the universe required for Typhonic workings.

• A bowl for divination. It should be small and flat and resemble the *Heb* bowl which Nepthys wears as a headdress. ⌣ This may be filled with a mixture of water and olive oil, ink, or wine, and provides a reflective surface for gazing when so filled.

• A stylus to inscribe lead or tin plates or carve figures on seashells. The stylus should be sharp and hard. The stylus should contain iron (the metal of Set) or steel. Bronze and copper, which are attuned to Isis and Horus, are to be avoided.

• Scissors or other instruments for cutting the papyrus. These need not be displayed on the altar, but they should be reserved for magical purposes. In addition to their practical function, they are a modern symbol of Set — corresponding to the *pesh-khent* knife used for cutting the umbilical cord and slaying the Apep monster. When using the scissors, the magician must strive to make him- or herself of the archetype of *Sutk* the isolator.

• Items which personalize the altar should be included to create a linkage of the personal manifestation (*ba*) of the magician and the divine forces she or he is seeking to immortalize his or her soul with. These could include an incense burner, a piece of meteoric iron, a photo of a teacher/initiator, a picture of the Big Dipper, etc. These items likewise should be hidden from profane eyes.

Items of short-term commitment. These are connected with the work at hand. Buying and maintaining these is a way of focusing on current endeavors.

• Papyrus. This wonderful paper is available at a large number of art shops and importers. Using it as part of the material to bind your spell to the material universe is one of the most effective methods of invoking the "feel" of the last age to be closely associated with Set-Typhon. This enables the beginning magician to "tap in" to those forces released in late antiquity, the magician in the middle of his/her development to *participate* in the tradition by subjectively traveling back to late antiquity, and the magician near the end of his/her evolution to begin to prepare for the casting forward of self. The use of a rare substance such as papyrus ensures little casual magic.

Papyrus should be scoured with a metal burnisher to make its fibers more compact and less absorbent.

• Inks and pens. Typhonic magic is best expressed with red ink. Experiment with the writing utensil preferred.

• Incenses. Frankincense, myrrh, and Egyptian incenses are generally burned as a "sacrifice" to the gods. Let your own taste be your guide, but look for natural rather than synthetic substances.

• Other writing materials such as lead, tin sheets, sea shells, etc. as needed for the work at hand.

The elements which sustain the magician. The processes and items suggested below are much more to be determined by the individual magician than those described above. They represent an attempt to re-create some of the psychological factors that the magician of late antiquity had. This is not an attempt to idolize or re-create that time. The postmodern Typhonian realizes that the ideas have grown stronger by their remanifestation. The postmodern Typhonian doesn't want a return to the past, in fact you'd probably only be able to pull the PC out of their cold dead fingers! But the postmodern Typhonian does want to attract the same sort of *ka* that empowered these magicians of the past. Here are some suggestions.

• Keep a diary. The *ba*, or that part of the soul responsible for continuity, must be very strong for dealing with the forces of magic. An understanding of who you are and where you are — as well as a record of your magical experiments — should be kept. Here you can write down your most intimate thoughts and hopes — perhaps even create a legacy to a magical son or daughter. Magic practiced without a strong sense of self leads to a downward spiral of catastrophe. Lucian's famous story of the "Sorcerer's Apprentice" of which Disney provided us an animated version in *Fantasia*, concerned an Egyptian apprentice in the Hermetic tradition of late antiquity. Know why you practice magic, and for what end. Observe its effect in your life. This will not take the place of initiation, which only passes from Mouth to Ear, but will allow you to provide as much light for your own journey as possible.

• Prepare for danger. The practitioners of the Hermetic tradition were in danger from the Roman government (especially their Christian agents in the fifth century). We live in a slightly more enlightened age, but there is still a tremendous prejudice against any practices not supported by the melting ice of monotheism. Be very careful who you speak to concerning your practice. Be vigilant of the safety of the outward manifestation of the *Tenemous* of your *Nous*. It is part of the Initiation of the Typhonian magician to be aware of his or her life-space and

45

protect it. In the beginning of the process it requires physical protection (from good locks to self defense) and psychological protection (healthy relationships with a good sense of psychological boundaries). This proceeds to temporal (investing for one's old age) and physical (making those groups strong you may need to call on, such as AMER.‡ Finally it means creating a legacy (from Initiating others to donating money to a library) that will help create a matrix for your remanifestation. If some neo-gestapo were to break in and take away everything at this moment — what have you committed to mind? Relax neither your vigilance nor your resolve.

• Nourish the intellect on the philosophical roots of the system, nourish the imagination with images of fantastic Egypt. Many occultnik books in "the Egyptian tradition" present predigested repeated glosses of the worst material available. Some of these even assert that you can gain wisdom by simply saying certain words. Real initiation seldom occurs during a rite. It more frequently occurs at the most unusual moments.

However, if you prepare your intellect with Plato, Plotinus, Iamblichus, Prophry — if your carry-along book is the *Meditations of Marcus Aurelius* — you will have a framework that will hold your gleaming gems of Initiation in a rationally accessible system.

Man doesn't live by philosophy alone. The rich inner life of day and night dreams to the most refined flights of aesthetic fancy are a needed part of the non-natural (spiritual) part of man. If you want the Gate of the South to open to you, you should surround yourself with those objects that appeal to your sense of Egypt. Put your scholarly and critical skills aside for a moment and indulge in the most unlikely (but fun) Egyptoid video. Let these images fill your imagination; they are no more nor less real than the battering media hype of a thousand cola ads. But these images sometimes provide a secret link to the Form they represent. Which the thousand colas won't.

• Observe festivals of Set-Typhon and make pilgrimages. Now, most of you are objecting that your calendar doesn't come marked with such festivals. What use are festivals anyway?

The festivals are times of re-birth. In the Egyptian language the words for Festival and Turning come from the same root, *heb.* The Typhonian magician celebrates festivals for three reasons. One, they separate him or her from the cultural matrix.

---

‡Alliance for Magical and Earth Religions, P. O. Box 16551, Clayton, MO 63105

Two, they provide times for gathering one's resources (counting your blessings) and begin a radical course correction toward your goals. Three, they connect the magician with certain moods and energies of another time.

Now the Egyptian calendars both Sothic and Civil were inaccurate. Therefore it is fairly easy to find different lists of when the Egyptian date corresponds to the current date. For the magician it is important to find a system pleasing to his/her sensibilities and stick with it. I prefer the translation of the Cairo Calendar published by Bob Brier in his *Ancient Egyptian Magic*, and my date for the birthday of Set comes from there. The Cairo Calendar dates from the XIXth-XXth, or "Setian," dynasties. The word "sacrifice" which appears in the following is *not* a bloody sacrifice. The Hermeticist in general (and the Typhonian Hermeticist in particular) does **not** seek to broaden the gap between gods and men by such practices as sacrifice, prayer, or bended knee. The Hermeticist always seeks to cross that gap and *act* as a god. The "sacrifices" are signs of power — both for yourself (How's your magic Working? Can you give more each year?) — and a way of unleashing forces on this Earth that further your divine goals.

I recommend four festivals for magicians attempting to associate themselves with, and to manipulate, the forces of the Typhonic tradition:

The Birthday of Set. July 29. Be sure you have a pleasant meal in the evening with friends and family. Give generously to those who most support you this day. The meal (if possible) should include foods sacred to Set: catfish, watermelon, some sort of endive or lettuce, pork. Sometime before midnight go to your altar, place the symbol of Set-Typhon on the four bricks, and say these words:

"O Set, son of Nuit, great of strength, hope of all hearts is thy name. Protection is at the hands of thy holiness. I am thy son/daughter. The name of this day is Naktab ("power of mind" or "strength of purpose"). I will rise in Might to be like you."

The Festival of Isadora. August 24. "Isadora" is a Greek compound name meaning "the gift of Isis." Isis is primarily the goddess of *preservation through recreation*. The last known hieroglyphic inscription was made on August 24, 394 CE by a priest of Isis at the Temple at Philae in Upper Egypt. Philae had been a well-known spot of Egyptian intellectual resistance during Ptolemaic times, and fittingly her Temple was the last to fall under the ice of monotheism. On the day of the last inscription we honor not only the priest, but that force of preservation which

47

has brought the treasures of magic from that Aeon to this. *Isis* represents the force which kept the ideas of Egypt preserved through cultural nurturing. Set, as *god of foreigners*, is the principal force for insuring those ideas exist outside of the cultural matrix of Egypt.

This festival may be celebrated with anyone who has a special affinity for the culture of late antiquity. The festival should include a few words in honor of that priest and of Isis as Goddess of the Manifest. Toasts may be drunk to historical teachers, and the spirits of the noble dead should be invited to share food with you as a precursor to their return to Earth. Words to be said:

"O Isis, great of Magic, we accept thy gift and swear to raise it to a new standard of excellence. O Isis, Great of Magic, whom Agathos Daimon permitted to rule in the entire Black Land. Your name is LOU LOULOU BATHARTHAR THARÊSIBATH ATHERNEKLÊSICH ATHERNEBOUNI ÊICHOMÔ CHOMÔTH/Isis-Sothis SOUÊRI, Boubastis, EURELIBAT CHAMARI NEBOUTOS OUÊRIAE ÊOA ÔAI. In thy holy name I honor your lector priest. Like him I carry the Scroll of Festival. Let your holy magics protect this place! Let your priests be born among us! Let the wisdom of the Black Land overcome its enemies!"

It is traditional to make a monetary sacrifice to an institution of Egyptological scholarship on this day.

The Festival of the Slaying of Osiris. October 16. On this day Osiris is entombed at Abydos. All the gods and goddesses who are fated to die (that is, all gods and goddesses save for Set) gather there to mourn. The Typhonian Hermeticist rejoices on this day, for it is the day of his or her triumph over the Cycles of Nature. The magician is advised to perform the traditional act of shattering a block of green faience which he has previously buried and mourned over. The fragments should be scattered in water. This re-enactment of the slaying of Osiris by Set was used to obtain a scepter of Djam (⌡). It is attested in the *Book of the Dead* (spell 125c). This is the first "Black Mass" in magical tradition.

These words should be directed to the West:

"I am ABLANATHANALBA, the griffin who holds Osiris in his hand. I am the fore-part of a lion. I am a leopard's tooth. I am ABRIAÔTH ALARPHÔTO SÊTH Ruler of the Kingdom of the Gods, whose First Thought did create and destroy the gods after my manner of coming into being. Thou dead one are OSORONOPHRIS, former ruler of the world. I look upon thee and I know I am deathless! I look upon thee and I know that I

48

will have victory over your minions! I look upon thee and send my weaknesses into your body to be buried! By the safe name MIRASU this is done. I hail the powerful daimon born this day, reflection of the First Thought! Hail, Daimon of this Day!"

Turn to the North and wait for a breeze from that direction to blow over you, then say:

"My father purifies me and I vow to overcome stasis. I choose χeper over Wen. My father gives me the scepter of the future, Djam, 'Giver of Winds' is its Name."

When performing outdoor rites, you should exercise caution in a non-friendly world.

The Day of Rebellion Set made against Osiris.

March 22. The Cairo Calendar urges that the name of Set not be spoken on this day lest it bring the disruptive energies of Set into one's household. The way of Shta-tu is the science of making the unknown known and the object of the knowing has a transformative effect on the subjective universe of the magician. If you know that you have invoked the forces of Set-Typhonic energies into your home, you will find them stimulating. Their very presence in your lair will cause it to be a place of physical and mental energy and will empower your work of seeking after the eternally Unmanifest. This Festival should be as loud an invocation of the names of Set-Typhon as is practical (different volume levels for the apartment dweller than the home owner). A monetary sacrifice should be made to a force that destabilizes the world in a positive way today. Words to be said:

"I call thee, Set-Typhôn, Baal, Ash, Teshub, Set of Dahlke, Set of Kharga, Set of Ombos, Set of Oxyrhynchus, KOLCHOI TONTONON SET, Lord APOMX PHRIOURIGX, BEPTU, powerful Typhon KOLCHLO PONTONON Set SACHAÔCH EA, IÔ BOLCHÔSÊTH IÔ ERBÊTH NEUTHI IAÔ IAÊ IÔSPHÊ IÔ IÔ ABRAÔTH, Set CHREPS, The Thunderer. Come from your seat behind the Thigh of the Bull. Come from SETHEUS where Grace and Word are joined. I am your son/daughter born of the seed of your mouth, born of your blood spilled in battle. Dwell here in this place which reflects the Temple of my mind! Dwell here and send forth your images and dreams! For as you pass near to me, I am ERBÊTH, and as you pass beyond, I remember myself and I am PAKERBÊTH. I am an isolate god, ever becoming. (Say seven times.)

In addition to these above festivals, which in their fourfoldness create a current of change running through both the magician's life and the world, the Typhonic Hermeticist should go

49

on the occasional pilgrimage. Now these pilgrimages can only be personally chosen. I will give examples of such activities. It is *essential* for Typhonians to associate themselves with new images and places. Stasis is the way of Osiris, and shunned by the magician seeking power in this world and knowledge of the next.

Here's an example of a pilgrimage. You visit the city of London. You perform a four-day rite. On the first day you visit the British Museum. You wander through the Egyptian gallery, the Greek rooms, whatever catches your fancy. You're awake and on the lookout for *Shta-tu* to manifest. When you've found whatever speaks to you, you silently interact with it as long as needed. On the second day you synthesize in your own mind the relationship between the mysterious object and your own life. On the third day you perform a rite of your own invention in which you enact the synthesis. On the fourth day you perform a rite of your own design casting your synthesis out into the world to join the stream of Typhonic revitalization — and you command your synthesis to return to you as a lever when you need it most. Until then let it create dreams and move the minds of others, or war against the Zeus, the personification of the stultifying norms of society.

I. Frame Rites

To perform the spells given in Chapter 6 of this book, you will need a ritual framework. The following frame rites are suggested, based on a factual understanding of the mechanics of Egyptian and Hermetic practices and an aesthetic derived from working with Set-Typhon in his current Aeon. You will wish to personalize these as your own research and practice will inform you in what needs to be done.

• If you have selected a spell, you will need to have assembled the material components for the spell ahead of time. Postmodern magicians DO NOT UNDER ANY CIRCUMSTANCES DO ANY ACTION THAT HARMS AN ANIMAL. If you know of any "magician" who harms animals in the course of his or her activities, you *must* as an ethical citizen report them to the appropriate authorities. If you decide to harm animals with your practices, know that I, Master of this Scroll, do command that every scourge and spell under ABLANATHANALBA harry and curse thee as long as thou dwellest on Earth.

• Wait till nightfall. Set, as god of the night sky, is best invoked by night.

• Take a cold shower. In the Egyptian language the word for "purity" and "cold" are the same. The "waters of purification"

50

were seen as flowing from the Seven Stars. Visualize the Seven Stars (the Big Dipper), imagine a cold water flowing from them washing away all illusions, all weakness — preparing you to ascend toward them.

• Dress for the work.

• Light the lamp. If you are reading from a papyrus, place it upon the four bricks.

• Facing the West, call to the four Typhonic Names (as follows) to begin the spiraling in of the Typhonic current which exists on this world. While facing the West, visualize a gigantic griffin which holds Osiris in his paws. Call him thus:

"ABLANATHANALBA, who holds Osiris in his paws, I call you to slay stasis!"

Turn to the South. Visualize a leopard standing by a waterfall. (Alternately, visualize an Eye in the middle of a storm cloud.)

"ERBÊTH, who causes ideas to be born, I call you to quicken minds with ideas yet unmanifest!"

Turn to the East. Visualize an ass-headed god holding iron knives.

"IÔ, who slays Apep, come to drive illusion from my mind and clear the way for the Real!"

Turn toward the North and visualize the Seven Stars. A dark Presence is behind them, vast and powerful.

"PAKERBÊTH, who gives the scepter of Djam called 'Giver of Winds', come to teach me how to be reborn as a god!"

• Now you are facing north and your altar is in front of you. Feel the energy spiraling into you. When you feel that the energy of the Typhonic Current of *this* world has reached its maximum, touch the symbol on your altar and say the Call to Set-Typhon:

"O mighty Sut-Hek, O Set-Typhon, O mighty Bepon-Beput-Bata, great in magic, I have brought thy enemy Osiris before thee in chains. I have wandered through the hollow of the cosmos OSORONOPHRIS seeking to perform deeds to your honor and my own. Necessity requires I perform this act of magic. Hasten quickly, quickly from thy starry solitude. I endeth thy exile. I know thee Typhon, Python, Set, IÔ ERBÊTH, IÔ PAKERBÊTH, IÔ BOLCHOSÊTH, IÔ APOMX, and You know Me.

"By your glance fresh from Setheus, the secret place, I Know my Unknown Soul. I Remember myself at this moment and my Soul is Immortalized, carried through the Seven Stars. In the Cycles of Four, Seven, and Nine do I bind this world in the rope of magic, create the *kaw* which sustain my will, and erect a

51

tenemous to my *nous* which liveth on with the days of Set-Typhon!

• At this moment allow power to stream into you. You may desire to perform an action that symbolizes the taking in of power.

• Look at the things on your altar. Invest them with meaning until they glow with magical life.

• Read the papyrus you have prepared.

• Feel free to add your own words concerning the work at hand. Speak as though the matter has already come to the resolution you desire.

• Now end the rite. You will send back the energy you have called to your chamber, but you will have Created more during the Rite. This too you will cast into the world. It does your will, and adds to the Typhonic stream. Firstly, address Set-Typhon. Visualize a streamer of energy going from you upward to the Seven Stars.

"Oh Akh of the Seven Stars, model of what I shall become, receive this gift of power. I praise thee Set-Typhon and thank thee for reminding me that I may act as a god while still alive. I will increase your Lore on the Earth and my Power in the Heavens through constant striving!"

Next, face each of the directions in reverse order. Let your energy stream out.

North:

"PAKERBÊTH, glorious Nine of the North, cause the stars you rule to be friendly to me as I am your friend."

East:

"IÔ, glorious Nine of the East, cause each dawning day to bring me further truths, as I help you to slay Apep."

South:

"ERBÊTH, glorious Seven of the South, cause new ideas to burn in me as I cause thee to burn with Life."

West:

"ABLANATHANALBA, glorious Eight of the West, make me steadfast in my resolve as I establish you over all of Osiris' domain."

• Then touch your Head.

"My thoughts are made strong by my will."

• Then touch your Heart.

"My feelings are made strong by my will."

• Then pass your hand over the four bricks.

"My world is made strong by my will."

- Closing statement

"What I have set in motion will advise and test me."

- Extinguish the Lamp. Take care of setting the room in order. When you have done so, leave the area and immerse yourself in an activity that will engage your interest. Speak to no one about the rite for at least 24 hours. At that time write down what you *remember* of the rite, and the reasons for its performance in your magical diary.

II. The Self-Initiation Rite

Spells of self-initiation, such as the one that follows or the Stele of Jeu the Hieroglyphist, are known as spells of seeking, or as spells of meeting/uniting. These spells generally allowed the magician to voyage to a place where effective knowledge could be directly obtained by the psyche. The Egyptian term is *seχenu*. This rare term is related to the verb *sχen*, to cleave, related to Set's birth when he tore himself from the goddess Neith. Such rites are not to be undertaken lightly, as they will tear you from the womb of the cosmos — the existing webwork of ideas and their magical links on this earth, and will end your career as a babe of the abyss.

This Rite should be performed *after* success with some of the spells in this book. Often in our magical practice, we will seize upon a fairly complicated "powerful looking" rite early on and lose its possible effectiveness. The immortalization of the psyche brings with it a certain power in the world. Indeed those who have accomplished such a level of Being seldom practice any form of external magic. However, most will believe themselves to be in this place of Being long before they have achieved it. These creatures fall to the two enemies of Set, stasis and delusion.

This ritual is a variation from the Mithraic initiation *PGM IV.*, 475-829. I recommend that the rite be performed once a year for seven years. Note the changes in your life and psyche at each performance. If the Rite hasn't filled you both with power and a burning desire, you are not a Child of Set, and this essence can not be made to grow in you.

Write the following on a papyrus. Perform the frame rite outlined above. Fill your censor with bryony, if available. Its acidic smell aids in cutting illusion.

At the appropriate time, read the words:

"I (insert magical name of the magician) rise from Earth where all stands forth in the Light of constant laws to the Seven Stars so that I may Order my own Becoming. I am a child of IÔ and I have the potential of Becoming like him, the Isolator. I

53

wander about the stars for I am one of them. SSSSSS. I go against the pull of the Sun and move toward the Seven Stars. They appear before me."

[Visualize the Seven Stars; each opens as a door and seven bull-headed gods step forth — one from each star. Behind them stand seven cobra-headed goddesses. You must hail each as follows.]

"Hail Guardians of the Pivot. I know Thee and Thou Know me. I speak freely with Thee and thus am unbound by seven fetters. When I return to Earth, I will have power greater than you who order the cycles of life and death.

"Hail to the First   AIERÔNTHI!
"Hail to the Second   MERCHEIMEROS!
"Hail to the Third   ACHRICHIOUR!
"Hail to the Fourth   MESARGILTÔ!
"Hail to the Fifth   CHICHRÔALITHÔ!
"Hail to the Sixth   ERMICHTHATHÔPS!
"Hail to the Seventh EORASICHÊ!

"O Montu, Lords of the Pole, you are the masques of Set in his exile, I need not speak to Thee for I am as one with Set!"

[The Lords of the Pole will vanish, but they will not forget you. They will appear to you as trials and tests on the world, but you will vanquish them in the end — their friction freeing you from internal fetters. Now you must address the seven cobra-headed goddesses. They will each bless you with a golden wand.]

"Hail to the First   CHREPSENTHAÊS!
"Hail to the Second   MENESCHEÊS!
"Hail to the Third   MECHRAN!
"Hail to the Fourth   ARAMACHÊS!
"Hail to the Fifth   ECHOMMIÊ!
"Hail to the Sixth   TICHNONDAÊS!
"Hail to the Seventh EROU ROMBRIÊS!

"I know that you Hathors have guarded the secret tradition until its rebirth. I am reborn with its knowledge and send you to others with my blessings!"

[The goddesses vanish, but they will remember your blessings and return to you at the most unlikely times with the gift of good advice. Now you must prepare yourself to meet Set. A darkness will form behind the stars and step forth as you speak.]

"O Mighty Lord, thou have been the Holy Headless One, AÔTH ABRAÔTH BASYM ISAK SABAÔTH IAÔ, thou hast been ATHELEBERSÊTH ABRASAX, thou hast been ABLANATHANABLA ERBÊTH IÔ PAKERBÊTH BOLCHÔSÊTH, thou hast been Satan and Mastemoth, thou hast been Ogo and Ninazu, thou hast been Rudra and the Elder Magician, thou hast been Aiwass and Tezcatlipoca, thou hast been Apedemak and Leviathan, thou hast been Belial and Tishpak, thou hast been the creator of all Aions, thou are now Set, the Mighty One who possesses the immortal fire. Speak to me, your son/daughter who comes from Earth."

[Speak now to Set in your own words and he will speak to you. Say the following spell.]

"My father Typhon KOLCHOI TONTONON Set, give me the scepter called 'Giver of Winds.'"

[Set presents thee with a *Djam* scepter; hold it in your right hand.]

"My father Typhon KOLCHOI TONTONON Set, give me the Ankh of reflection."

[Set presents it. Hold the ankh in your left hand.]

"Allow me to swallow your wisdom so that I may remember it as my own."

[Fire flies out of Set's Mouth and into yours. You will swallow it and Set returns behind the seven stars.]

"The god in my heart was χephra and I saw Infinite Space. The god in my heart was Ma'at and I saw Beauty. The god in my heart was Shuti and I saw Yesterday-Tomorrow. The god in my heart was Geb and I saw the place to erect my Temple. The god in my heart was Nuit and I saw how to create a world. The god in my heart was Osiris and I saw how to sink within and gather strength. The god in my heart was Set and I saw how to preserve the force of mind. The god in my heart was Isis and I saw how to re-shape in accordance with all my Secrets. The god in my heart was Nepthys and I learned how to create Time. I look down upon the whole of the Earth and her secrets open to me. Every spell and scourge is obedient to me! I am KATATOU OUSIRI. I am ABERAMENTHÔOU. I will return to this secret region as a Bennu-bird!"

[Now visualize your return to Earth, to your continent, nation, city, home, body. For a moment think of all that you must do, of the challenges in your life, then say the following.]

"I have equipped myself like Set Great-in-Magic, who passes now through the whole of the world. Nothing is lacking in me, nothing ceases that I put in motion. I am more glorious, more powerful than the gods of the Two Lands. I have cleaved the Night and I am reborn. I am equipped like Set who mightily broke forth."

Chapter 6
Spells

I. Greek Spells

A Spell for the Workshop
(including the recipe for Typhonian ink)
PGM XII. 96-106

Himerios' recipes:
Drawing made with Typhonian ink: A fiery red poppy, juice from an artichoke, seed of the Egyptian acacia, red Typhon's ocher, unslaked quicklime, wormwood with a single stem, gum, rainwater.

To do well at the workshop: On the egg of a male bird write and then bury the egg near the threshold where you live. "CHPYHRIS, egg, which is CHORBAI SANACHARSÔ AMOUN ⊬ SPHÊ SPHÊ GAKNEPHÊ SIETHÔ ⊬ NOUSI NOUSI, you are the sacred egg from birth, which is SELBIOUS BATHINI PHNIÊIAÊO AÔÊ AÔÊ AÔIAÔI A PHIAEA THÔUTH IAÔ SELETÊA THEÔÊPH OXYMBRÊ ÊÊÊ III."

The oration concerning the egg: "Great God, give favor, business to me and to this place where the egg lies, in the house I do my business, SELEPEL THEÔEPH and Good Daimon, send to this place every business and good daily profit. You are my work. You are the great Ammon, who dwells in heaven. Come, help me."

Notes: CHPYHRIS is a Greek form of χeper. The egg of a male bird is a pottery egg, which symbolizes *potential* becoming locked in craft. The egg is a symbol of the Unnamed God within. The ingredients of the ink provide several clues to Set-Typhon's nature.

Spell for Obtaining Luck from Set
PGM IV. 154-285

·Nephotes to Psammetichos, immortal king of Egypt. Greetings. Since the great god has appointed you immortal king and nature has made you the best wise man, I too, with a desire to show you the industry in me, have sent you this magical procedure which, with complete ease, produces a holy power. And after you have tested it, you too will be amazed at the miraculous nature of this magical operation. You will observe through bowl divination on whatever day or night you want, in whatever place you want, beholding the god in the water and hearing a voice from the god which speaks in verses in answer to whatever you want. You will attain both the ruler of the universe and whatever you command, and he will speak on other matters which you ask about. You will succeed by inquiring in this way: First, attach yourself to Helios in this manner: At whatever sunrise you want, go up to the highest part of the house and spread a pure linen garment on the floor. Do this with a mystagogue. But as for you, crown yourself with dark ivy while the sun is in mid-heaven, at the fifth hour, and while looking upward lie down naked on the linen and order your eyes to be completely covered with a black band. And wrap yourself like a corpse, close your eyes and, keeping your direction toward the sun, begin these words.

Prayer:

"O Mighty Typhon, ruler of the realm
Above and master, god of gods, O lord
ABERAMENTHÔOU (see note below)
O dark's disturber, thunder's bringer, whirlwind,
Night-flasher, breather-forth of hot and cold,
Shaker of rocks, wall-trembler, boiler of
The waves, disturber of the sea's great depth, IÔ ERBÊT
    AU TAUI MENI,
I'm He who searched with you the whole world and
Found great Osiris, whom I brought you chained.
I'm He who joined you in war against the gods.
I'm She who closed heaven's double gates and put
To sleep the serpent which must not be seen,
Who stopped the seas, the streams, the river currents
Where'er you rule this realm. And as your soldier
I have been conquered by the gods, I have
Been thrown face down because of empty wrath.
But in my wrath I conquered the gods within,
And have awakened for a season. I rise up
That we may work our will together on this Earth.
AEMINAEBARÔTHERRETHÔRABEANIMEA,
O grant me power, I beg, and give to me
This favor, so that, whensoe'er I tell
One of the gods to come, he is seen coming
Swiftly to me in answer to my chants,
NAINE BASANAPTATOU EAPTOU MENÔPHAESME
PAPTOU MENÔPH AESIME TRAUAPTI PEUCHRE TRAUARA
PTOUMEPH MOURAI ANCHOUCHAPHAPTA MOURSA

58

ARAMEI IAÔ ATHTHARAUI MENOKER BORO PTOUMETH AT
TAUI MENI CHARCHARA PTOUMAU LALAPSA TRAUI
TRAUESPSE MAMÔ PHORTOUCHA AEEIO IOY OEÔA EAI
AEEI ÔI IAÔ AEI AI IAÔ."

After you have said this three times, there will be this sign
of divine encounter, but you, armed by having this magical soul,
be not alarmed. For a sea falcon flies down and strikes you on
the body with its wings, signifying this: that you should arise.
But as for you, rise up and clothe yourself with white garments
and burn on an earthen censer uncut incense in grains while
saying this:

"I have been attached to your holy form.
I have been given power by your holy name.
I have acquired your emanation of the gods,
Lord, god of gods, master, daimon.
ATHTHOUIN THOUTHOUI TAUANTI LAÔ
APTATÔ."

Having done this, return as lord of a godlike nature which is
accomplished through this divine encounter.

Inquiry of bowl divination and necromancy:
Whenever you want to inquire about matters, take a bronze
vessel, either a bowl or saucer, whatever kind you wish. Pour
water: rainwater if you are calling upon heavenly gods, seawater
if gods of the earth, river water if Osiris or Sarapis, spring water
if the dead. Holding the vessel on your knees, pour out green
olive oil, bend over the vessel and speak the prescribed spell.
And address whatever god you want and ask about whatever
you wish, and he will reply to you and tell you about anything.
And if he has spoken dismiss him with the spell of dismissal,
and you who have used this spell will be amazed.

The spell spoken over the vessel is: "AMOUN
AUANTAU LAIMOUTAU RIPTOU MANTAUI IMANTOU
LANTOU LAPTOUMI ANCHÔMACH ARAPTOUMI, hither to me,
O Setnakt, O Nya; appear to me this very hour and do not
frighten my eyes. Hither to me, O Setnakt, O Nya, be attentive
to me because he wishes and commands this ACHCHÔR
ACHCHÔR ACHACHACH PTOUMI CHACHCHÔ
CHARACHÔCH CHAPTOUME CHÔRACHARACHÔCH
APTOUMI MECHÔCHAPTOU CHARACHPTOU CHACHCHÔ
CHARACHÔ PTENACHÔCHEU" (a hundred letters in Greek).‡

---

‡αχχωρ αχχωρ αχαχαχ πτουμι χαχχω χαραχωχ χαπτουμη
χωραχαραχωχ απτουμι μηχωχαπτου χαραχπτου χαχχω χαραχω
πτεναχωχευ

But you are not unaware, mighty king and leader of magicians, that this is the chief name of Typhon, at whom the ground, the depths of the sea, Hades, heaven, the sun, the moon, the visible chorus of stars, the whole universe all tremble, the name which, when it is uttered, forcibly brings gods and daimons to it. This is the name that consists of 100 letters. Finally, when you have called, whomever you called will appear, god or dead man, and he will give an answer about anything you ask. And when you have learned to your satisfaction, dismiss the god merely with the powerful name of the hundred letters as you say, "Depart, master, for the great god, [insert magical or deified name of magician], wishes and commands this of you." Speak the name, and he will depart. Let this spell, mighty king, be transmitted to you alone, guarded by you, unshared.

There is also the protective charm itself which you wear while performing, even while standing: onto a silver leaf inscribe this name of 100 letters with a bronze stylus, and wear it strung on a thong from the hide of an ass.

Divine encounter of the divine procedure: Toward the rising sun say:

"I call you who did first control gods' wrath,
You who hold royal scepter o'er the heavens,
You who are midpoint of the stars above,
You, master Typhon, you I call, who are
The dreaded sovereign o'er the firmament,
You who are fearful, awesome, threatening,
You who're obscure and irresistible
And hater of the wicked, you I call,
Typhon, in hours unlawful and unmeasured,
You who've walked on unquenched, clear-
        crackling fire,
You who are over snows, below dark ice,
You who hold sovereignty over the Moirai,
I invoked you in pray'r, I call, almighty one.
That you perform for me whate'er I ask
Of you, and that you nod assent at once
To me and grant that what I ask be mine

(add the usual), because I adjure you GAR THALA BAUZAU THÔRTHÔR KATHAUKATH IATHIN NA BORKAKAR BORBA KARBORBOCH MÔ ZAU OUZÔNZ ÔN YABITH, mighty Typhon, hear me, [insert name of magician], and perform for me [insert short description of desired result, both factual and tempered by the inspirational/artistic state of the magician]. For I speak your true names, IÔ ERBÊTH IÔ PAKERBÊTH IÔ

60

BOLCHOSÊTH OEN TYPHON ASBARABÔ BIEAISE ME NERÔ
MARAMÔ TAUER CHTHENTHÔNIE ALAM BETÔR
MENKECHRA SAUEIÔR RESEIODÔTA ABRESIOA PHÔTHER
THERTHÔNAX NERDÔMEU AMÔRES MEEME ÔIES SYSCHIE
ANTHÔNIE PHRA; listen to me and perform [repeat the
description]."

Notes: The magician claims to have done all of Set-Typhon's
deeds on this Earth — and asks for a generalized increase in
power and luck. This spell should only be performed by a
master who, having *obtained* power in the world through ending
stasis and overcoming delusion, is ready for an increase in power.
This is the most Hellenic of all the spells associated with Set-
Typhon, firstly for its reference to XXVIth dynasty kings and
secondly for its mention of the Greek "Sarapis."

The ABERAMEN formula is a long palindrome with "A"
(*alpha*) on each end. Like all such, it pulls the dynamic emotional
memories of the magician and pits them against the static
unfeeling present. It is related to the ABLANATHANALBA
formula, but it is hinged on "N" (= Scorpio) rather than TH (=
Aethyr). See Flowers' *Hermetic Magic* for deciphering such
formulas. It is a name of Toth and Montu. The formula is:
ABERAMENETHÔOUTHLERTHEXANAXETHRELTHUOÔTHENEM
AREBA

Arkte Spell for General Empowerment
PGM IV. 1331-89
**Powerful spell of the Bear which accomplishes
anything:** Have your herbalist compound an oil that is strongly
musky and fiery (preferably with Egyptian cumin). Offer some of
the oil to the Bear goddess who rules the Seven Stars, by
pouring a small amount on the ground while looking at Ursa
Major, saying: "ARKTE is your name. Judgment is your name.
Fierce is your nature. You are as a lioness protecting her whelps.
In essence I am the same." After you have made this offering
create a cord of black and red yarn to wrap around your head.
As you plait the strands together think of tying in the vitality of
a black bull, the stubbornness of a black ass and the persistence
of a she-goat. Place the cord around your head. If you are a man,
place a second cord around your phallus as well. Anoint all of
your body with the oil, especially your lips. Face the North and
say the following words, but freely add anything that comes of
your own inspiration:

61

"I call upon you, holy, very powerful, very-glorious, very-strong, holy autochthons, assistants of the great god, the powerful chief daimons, you who are inhabitants of Chaos, of Erebos, of the abyss, of the depth, of earth, dwelling in the recesses of heaven, lurking in the nooks and crannies of houses, shrouded in dark clouds, watchers of things not to be seen, leaders of those in the underworld, administrators of the infinite, wielding power over earth, earth-shakers, foundation-layers, servants in the chasm, shudderful fighters, fearful ministers, turning the spindle, freezing snow and rain, air-transversers, causing summer heat, wind-bringers, lords of Fate, inhabitants of dark Erebos, bringers of compulsion, sending flames of fire, bringing snow and dew, wind-releasers, disturbers of the deep, treaders on the calm sea, mighty in courage, grievers of the heart, powerful potentates, cliff-walkers, adverse daimons, iron-hearted, wild-tempered, unruly, guarding Tartaros, misleading Fate, all-seeing, all-hearing, all-subjecting, heaven-walkers, spirit-givers, living simply, heaven-shakers, gladdening the heart, those who join together death, revealers of angels, punishers of mortals, sunless revealers, rulers of daimons, air-transversers, almighty, holy, unconquerable AÔTH ABAÔTH BASYM ISAK SABAÔTH IAÔ IAKÔP MANARA SKORTOURI MORTROUM EPHRAULA THREERSA; do [insert short description of desired result, both factual and tempered by the inspirational /artistic state of the magician]."

Then write on a piece of papyrus the hundred-lettered name of Typhon, curved as a star, and bind it in the middle of the core with the letters showing.

This is the name: ACHCHÔR ACHCHÔR
ACHACHACHPTOUMI CHACHCHÔ CHARACHÔCH
CHAPTOUME CHÔRA CHÔCH APTOUMIME CHÔCHAPTOU
CHARACHPTOU CHACHCHÔ CHARA CHÔCH
PTENACHÔCHEOU.‡

Note: This is the shape of the star ⚔ taken from the mason's marks of Setian work crews who built the tomb of Seti I.

---

‡In Greek: αχχωρ αχχωρ αχαχαχπτουμι χαχχω χαραχωχ
χαπτουμη χωρα χωχ απτουμιμη χωχαπτου χαραχπτου χαχχω
χαρα χωχ πτεναχωχεου

Rite of the Headless One
(According to Jeu)
PGM V. 96-172

To prepare for this rite, write the following words on a strip of clean papyrus, with the beneficial sign on each side of the words pointing leftward. This is the Sign:

These are the words:
AÔTH ABRAÔTH BASYM ISAK SABAÔTH IAÔ

Wrap the strip around your head from temple to temple. Face the North and visualize the strip as a serpent swallowing its own tail, as you say the six names imagine your mind growing outward to the limit of consciousness/the universe. When the serpent around your head is the same size as the universe, say the following:

"Subject to me all daimons, so that they obey me whether they are of the Mind, or the Fates of heaven, or the air, or the earth, or beneath the earth. I am seeing the Absolute and henceforth every spell and scourge will work my will.

"I summon you, Headless One, who created earth and heaven, who created night and day, you who created light and darkness; you are Osoronnophris whom none has ever seen; you are Iabas; you are Iapos; you have distinguished the just and the unjust; you have made female and male; you have revealed seed and fruits; you have made men love each other and hate each other.

"I am Moses your prophet to whom you have transmitted your mysteries celebrated by Israel; you have revealed the moist and the dry and all nourishment; hear me.

"I am the messenger of Pharaoh Osoronnophris; I will speak your true name which has been transmitted to the prophets of Israel. Hear me, ARBATHIAÔ REIBET ATHELEBERSÊTH ARA BLATHA ALBEU EBENPHCHI CHITASGOÊ IBAÔTH IAÔ; listen to me and turn away that which is moved to appear against me.

"I call upon you, awesome and invisible god with an empty spirit, AROGOGOROBRAÔ SOCHOU MODORIÔ PHALARCHAÔ OOO. Holy Headless One, deliver me, [insert magical name of magician], from the daimon which restrains me, ROUBRIAÔ MARI ÔDAM BAABNABAÔTH ASS ADÔNAI APHNIAÔ ITHÔLÊTH ABRASAX AÊÔÔY; mighty Headless One, deliver me, NN, from the daimon which restrains me. MABARRAIÔ IOÊL KOTHA ATHORÊBALÔ ABRAÔTH, deliver me, [insert magical name of magician] AÔTH ABRAÔTH BASYM ISAK SABAÔTH IAÔ.

"He is the lord of the gods; he is the lord of the inhabited world; he is the one whom the winds fear; he is the one who made all things by the command of his voice.

"Lord, King, Master, Helper, preserve in me my illuminated knowledge, IEOU PYR IOU PYR IAÔT IAÊÔ IOOU ABRASAX SABRIAM OO YY EY OO YY ADÔNAIE, quickly, quickly, good messenger of God ANLALA LAI GAIA APA DIACHANNA CHORYN.

"I am the headless daimon with my sight in my feet; I am the mighty one who speaks the Word of the immortal fire; I am the act of revealing truth who hates the fact that unjust deeds are done in the world; I am the one who makes the lightning flash and speaks its name in the thunder roll; I am the one whose sweat falls upon the earth as rain so that it can inseminate it; I am the one whose mouth burns completely; I am the one who begets and destroys; I am the Favor of the Aion; my name is a heart encircled by a serpent; great is my might, greater still my might through you."

Notes: This complex rite combines Greek, Hebrew, and Egyptian ideas. The petitioner begins by invoking the god, then Becoming the god. From the God he receives a *Nomos*, a divine law which the earth will be bound into fulfilling as soon as the Magician can articulate the Law. This rite is based on ideas of Moses as divine lawgiver and prophet as presented in the great Hebrew-Platonic-Stoic synthesis of Philo of Alexandria's *Vita Mosis*. Philo grafted two ideas on the cult of the Magus. First, that the superior magician represented a *Logos* (Word) and articulated the *Nomos* (Law or Foundation) of that Logos. Second, that the superior magician did not go into an ecstatic trance — but received the Divine knowledge in a way that he could read it.

Philo's early first century work created the legend of the Jews as Magicians for both Egyptians and Greeks. (For an in-depth study of the *Vita Mosis*, see "Arcana Mundi: Prophecy and Divination in the *Vita Mosis* of Philo of Alexandria" in *The Ancient World Mystery Cults in Late Antiquity*, Vol XXVI, Num. 2, 1995.)

The attribution of this text to Jeu, a Gnostic teacher who taught methods of divine ascent through the use of sigils, is telling. Jeu taught his disciples how to enter the Secret Place (Setheus) and obtain there the knowledge to create Aeons. This spell in Greek and the books of Jeu in Coptic were both written 350-440 CE. Both contain the idea of an "empty spirit" formed by the actions of ascending and descending from the place of internal initiation. This empty, invisible, holy, or "future" spirit is the unique place from which each magician steps out of the Cosmos to work his will upon it.

The Greek formulas on the papyrus consist of secret names for the Jewish God — the whole strip contains 24 characters in Greek beginning with Alpha and ending with Omega.

The "Holy Headless One" is identified in other texts as being behind the constellation Draco. He is Set in his form of the Bata serpent. Bata exists either as a continuous serpent, or a series of Remanifestations (see "The Tale of Two Brothers"). Esoterically these are the same — as are Being and Becoming.

Because this rite does *not* produce ecstasy, but rather a slow unfolding of the Law — it requires many performances. Once an individual has found his or her law, all magic works for them — there is no longer any lack of harmony within.

A note on the Names: The Samaritan forms of *IAO, Iabas,* and *Iapos*, which are rather rare for the magical papyri, suggest that the author of this spell was the Sethian gnostic Dositheous, the Samaritan magician who was the author of the great Sethian gospel known as the *Three Steles of Seth*, and teacher of Simon Magus. He likely introduced — or revealed from older sources — the myth of the Scarlet Woman.

Spell for a Magical Servant
PGM XI.a 1-40

Apollonius of Tyana's old serving woman: Take Typhon's skull (traditionally an ass: find a personal symbol of fixity of purpose, a memento of a cherished ancestor who was as stubborn as the day is long is a good start) and write the following characters in black paint:

" ⌐∤⊠ ⊙ ⌐ ⊀   SABERRA."

Then, going to a suitable place, by a river, the sea, or at the
fork of a road, in the middle of the night put the "skull" on the
ground, place it under your left foot, and speak as follows.

   The formula: "ERITHYIA MEROPÊ GERGIRÔ CHÊTHIRA
ANAPEROUCHETH LYRÔPHIA GÊGETHIRA LOLYN
GOUGÔGÊ AMBRACHA BITH AEBILÊ MARITHAIA
MPROUCHE ABÊL ETHIRAÔ APAOTH ÔCHORIÊLA
MÔRÊTHIRA PHECHIRÔ ÔSRI PHOIRA AMERIPHRE PHÊ.
OUTHÊRA GARGERGIÔ TITHEMYMÊ MÊRAPSÊCHIR AÔRIL.
Come, appear, O goddess called the Mistress of the House."

   After you say this, you will behold sitting on an ass a
woman of extraordinary loveliness, possessing a heavenly beauty,
indescribably fair and youthful. As soon as you see her, make
obeisance and say: "I thank you, lady for appearing to me. Judge
me worthy of you. May your Majesty be well disposed to me.
And accomplish whatever task I impose on you."

   The goddess will reply to you, "What do you have in mind?"
   You say, "I have need of you for domestic service."
   At that, she will get off the ass, shed her beauty, and will be
an old woman. And the old woman will say to you, "I will serve
and attend you."

   After she tells you this, the goddess will again put on her
own beauty, which she had just taken off, and she will ask to be
released.

   But you say to the goddess, "No, lady! I will use you until I
get her."

   As soon as the goddess hears this, she will go up to the old
lady, and will take her molar tooth and a tooth from the ass and
give both to you; and after that it will be impossible for the old
woman to leave you, unless perhaps you want to release her.
From that time forth, you will receive a bounty of great benefits,
for everything that your soul desires will be accomplished by
her. She will guard all your possessions and in particular will
find out for you whatever anyone is thinking about you.

   Indeed she will tell you everything and will never desert
you: such is her store of good will toward you. But if ever you
wish, there is a way to release her (but never do this!). Take her
tooth and the ass's tooth, make a bonfire, and throw them into
the fire, and with a shriek the old woman will flee without a
trace. Do not be prone to release her, since it will be impossible
for you to replace her.

66

But do release the goddess, when you are sure that the old woman will serve you, by speaking as follows: "MENERPHER PHIÊ PRACHÊRA LYLÔRI MÊLICHARÊ NÊCHIRA." When the old woman hears this, the goddess will mount the ass and depart.

The phylactery to be used throughout the rite: The skull of the ass. (Again, visualize this.) Fasten the ass's tooth with silver and the old lady's tooth with gold, and wear them always; for if you do this, it will be impossible for the old woman to leave you. The rite has been tested.

Note: "Mistress of the House" = Nepthys. Of course, this spell is not about materializing some servant in the objective universe, but of causing some aspects of your human software to become automatically supportive of your higher goals.

Spell for Causing a Break Up
PDM XII. 365-75

Charm for causing separation: On a pot for smoked fish inscribe a spell with a bronze stylus and recite it afterwards and put it where they (your victims) are, where they usually return, repeating at the same time this spell: "I call upon you, god, you who are in the empty air, you who are terrible, invisible, and great, you who afflict the earth and shake the universe, you who love disturbances and hate stability and scatter the clouds from one another, IAIA IAKOUBIAI IÔ ERBÊTH, IÔ PAKERBÊTH IÔ BOLCHOSÊTH BASDOUMA PAPATHNAX APOPSS OSESRÔ ATAPH THATBRAOU EÔ THATHTHABRA BÔRARA AROBREITHA BOLCHOSÊTH KOKKOLOIPTOLÊ RAMBITHNIPS: give to him, [insert name of male target], the son of her, [insert name of male target's mother], strife, war; and to him, [insert name of male target], the son of her, [insert name of male target's mother], odiousness, enmity, just as Typhon and Osiris had" (but if it is a husband and wife, "just as Typhon and Isis had"). "Strong Typhon, very powerful one, perform your mighty acts."

Notes: Fish are sacred to Typhon — any culturally taboo object will do. Likewise ink may replace the bronze stylus — in all matters, let your common sense of cultural signs guide you.

Another Spell of Separation
PDM XII. 62-75 [PGM XII. 449-52]

Take a piece of pottery. Write the names of the two people you want to separate on it. Break the shard in two pieces. Say the spell below. Bury the pieces in the road in front of the targets' home. Bury one to the right and one to the left. If you wish, write the names on parchment and tear it into two pieces.

Formula: BRAG GRAB BRAGH HÔSPERTHNAKS BHRIENTHE(?)GH BASPHETHÔI ATHRYPH PATATHNAG APÔPSI IÔ-BÊTH IÔ-BÔLGHÔSÊTH IÔ-PAGERBÊTH, separate [insert name of male target] born of [insert name of male target's mother], from [insert name of female target] born of [insert name of female target's mother]!" After repeating the formula twice, draw this figure:

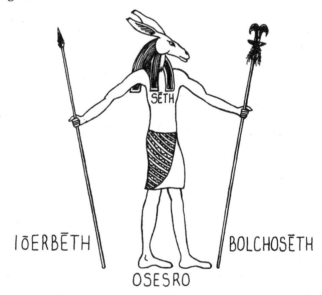

"Separate [insert name of male target] born of [insert name of male target's mother], from [insert name of female target] born of [insert name of female target's mother]!" And you say this name to it again, seven times. Bury the shard where they will walk over it.

Note the alternative spelling of the names — this represents another attempt to take verbal formulas and write them down. The written word was the key to survival and transmission of knowledge. Notice the alternative spellings of PAGERBÊTH, etc.

68

A Third Spell of Separation
PDM XII. 50-61 [PGM XII. 445-48]

Take a sheet of papyrus and write the spell below on it. Wrap something foul inside — crocodile dung if you have it handy, but anything nasty will do. After you have said the spell over it— hide it near the targets' doorway.

Here are the names to be written on it and you recite them over it also, seven times: "IÔ-ERBÊTH IÔ-SÊTH IÔ-BÔLGHÔSÊTH IÔ-PAGERBÊTH IÔ-PATATHNAGS LÊEMENG.RÊ IO-ÔSESRO IÔ-GHLÔNTOÊPS, separate [insert name of male target] born of [insert name of male target's mother], from [insert name of female target] born of [insert name of female target's mother]!" It is needful for the great workings of my being that they separate. "Separate Isis from Typhon, may they become as repelling magnets freeing (her/him) for my attraction."

Note: Any spell of separation may be used to remove a person from a group, corporation, etc. If you find that you make fequent use of this sort of sorcery, your life probably isn't under control.

Request for a Dream Oracle
PGM VII. 359-369

Take a strip of clean linen and write on it the following name. Roll it up to make a wick, pour pure olive oil over it and light it.

The formula to be written is this: "HARMIOUTH LAILAM CHÔOUCH ARSENOPHRÊ PHRÊU PHTHA HARCHENTECHTHA."

In the evening then, when you are about to go to sleep, being pure in every respect, do this: Go to the lamp, say seven times the following formula, extinguish the lamp and go to sleep.

The formula to be spoken is as follows: "SACHMOUNE PAÊMALIGOTÊRÊÊNCH, the one who shakes, who thunders, who has swallowed the serpent, surrounds the moon, and hour by hour raises the disk of the sun, 'CHTHETNÔNI' is your name. I ask you, lord of the gods, SÊTH CHRÊPS: reveal to me concerning the things I wish."

Note: Take good care of your diet and exercise for a week before this spell. Sleep alone and have writing or recording instruments nearby to record your vision. Such visions may be hard to interpret and will tend to serve your long-term goals — which you may not have rationally discovered yet.

Spell to Cause Insomnia
PGM VII. 652-60

Say this spell over red ink. "You are the Essence of the Goat of Mendes. Ever awake. Ever vigilant. Hypnos flees from you. You are as alert as Re." Use the consecrated ink to write the following words on the right wing of a paper figure of a bat: "BÔRPHÔR PHORBA PHORPHARBA PHÔRBÔRPHORBA PHORBA PHORBA PHORBA BAPHAIÊ PHÔRBAPHÔR BARBA" Write these words on the left wing: "PHÔRPHÔR PHORBA BORPHOR PHORBA BORPHOR PHORBA PHORPHOR PHORBABÔR BORBORBA PHÔRPHÔR PHORBA" (likewise, add the usual as you want).

Note: If you wish to use the spell offensively, visualize the bat flying to your victim and attaching itself to his or her face. If you wish to use the spell to keep yourself awake— simply state aloud the reasons you need to be awake for your goals of self-development.

A Charm to Restrain Anger and Cause Slavish Love
PGM VII. 940-68

On clean papyrus write with pure myrrh ink these names together with the "stele":

IÔERBÊTH	IÔPAKERBÊTH
IÔERBÊ	ÔPAKERBÊTH
IÔERB	PAKERBÊTH
IÔER	AKERBÊTH
IÔE	KERBÊTH
IÔ	ERBÊTH
I	RBÊTH
	BÊTH
	ÊTH
	TH

IÔSESESRÔ	
ÔSESESRÔ	
SESESRÔ	
ESESRÔ	IÔPÊMPS
SESRÔ	ÔPÊMPS
ESRÔ	PÊMPS
SRÔ	ÊMPS
RÔ	MPS
Ô	PS

70

"Come to me, you who are in the everlasting air, you who are invisible, almighty, creator of the gods. Come to me, you who are the unconquerable daimon. Come to me, you who are never grieved for your brother, Seth. Come to me, you fire-bright spirit. Come to me, you god who are not to be despised, you daimon, and put to silence, subordinate, enslave him, [name of target], to him, [name of person that the spell is being performed for], and cause him to come under my feet.

Notes: This spell will summon the Elder Horus, brother of Set who brings sovereignty over its intended target. This spell may be modified to effect deep social change.

Restraining Charm
PGM XXXVI. 1-34

Works on everything. Taking a lead lamella, hammered out while cold, inscribe with a bronze stylus the creature below and the names, and deposit it nearby and in front the person: "Come Typhon, who sit on the underworld gate; IÔ ERBÊTH, who killed his own brother, IÔ PAKERBÊTH IÔ BOLCHOSÊTH IÔ APOMPS IÔ SESENRÔ IÔ BIMAT IAKOYMBIAI ABERRAMENTHÔOY LERTHEXANAX ETHRELYOÔTH MEMAREBA, of Seth, BOLKOL, fear your uninhibited son."

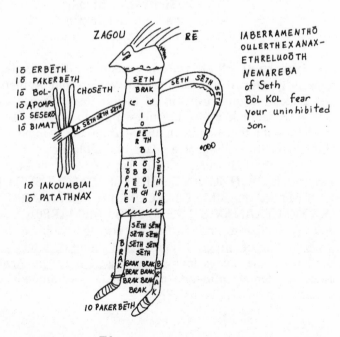

Note: BOLKOL = Baal of Kharga, the Oasis where the wine called the "Gift of Set" was made. *KoL* is a nickname meaning Libia.

Spell for Sexual Attraction
PGM XXXIIa. 1-25

"As Typhon is the adversary of Helios, so inflame the heart and soul of that [insert name of target] whom [insert name of target's mother] bore, even from her own womb, ADÔNAI ABRASAX PINOUTI and SABAÔS; burn the soul and heart of that [insert name of target] whom [insert name of target's mother] bore, for love of me whose mother [insert name of magician's mother] bore, now, now; quickly, quickly."

"In this same hour and on this same day, from this moment on, mingle together the souls of both and cause that [insert name of target] whom [insert name of target's mother] bore to be this Serapiakos whom Threpte bore, through every hour, every day and every night. Wherefore, ADÔNAI, loftiest of gods, whose name is the true one, carry out the matter, ADÔNAI."

Notes: Typhon has a particular enmity toward Apollo who slew him in his form of Python. All sulfur springs and places of boiling water have strong Typhonic currents.

Spell for Strong
Sexual Attraction
PGM XXXVI. 69-101

Love spell of attraction, excellent inflamer, than which none is greater. It attracts men to women and women to men and makes virgins rush out of their homes. Take a pure papyrus and with red ink write the following names and figure, and touch it with the magical material from the woman you desire. Hide it on the ceiling of a place of Indulgence.

Write the following: "Come, Typhon, who sit on top of the gate, IÔ ERBÊTH IÔ PAKERBÊTH IÔ BALCHOSÊTH IÔ APOMPS IÔ SESENRÔ IÔ BIMAT IAKOUMBIAI ABERRAMENTHÔ OULERTHEXANAX ETHRELUOÔTH MEMAREBA TOU SÊTH, as you are in flames and on fire, so also the soul, the heart of her, [insert name of target] whom [insert name of target's mother] bore, until she comes loving me, [insert name of magician], and glues her female pudenda to my male one, immediately, immediately; quickly, quickly."

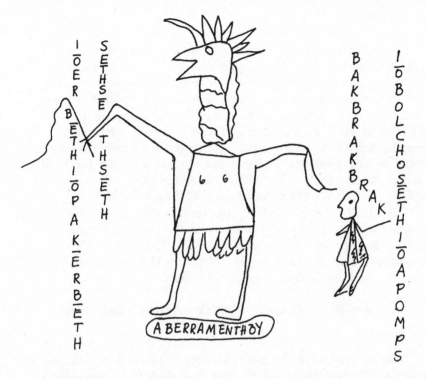

Note: All magic, then as now, consists of sending signals. If your Will is not strong, the spell will never make it beyond your own soul-body complex and you'll be a whole lot hornier than before. Many men and women thinking themselves great magicians have destroyed their lives with love spells.

Double Quick Action Sex Spell
PGM VII. 300a-310

Take a seashell and write the holy names in red ink.
Spell: "I adjure you, shell, by bitter Necessity (MASKELLI formula) and by those fates who have been placed in charge of the Punishments, LAKI LAKIÔ LAKIMOU MOUKILA KILAMOU IÔR MOUÔR MOUDRA MAXTHA MOUSATHA: attract her, [insert name of target] whom [insert name of target's mother] bore" (add the usual, whatever you wish). "Do not be stubborn, but attract her, OUCH OUCH CHAUNA MOUCHLIMALCHA MANTÔR MOURKANA MOULITHA MALTHALI MOUI EIEI YYY AE AIE YOÔ AEI AEI AEI AÔA AÔA AÔA IAÔ ÔAI ÔAI

73

AIÔ ÔIA IÔA IAÔ ÔAI, attract her, [insert name of target]" (add the usual). As the moon waxes in Aries or Taurus add the usual, whatever you wish.

Notes: The Maskelli formula contains names of Hekate, Erskighal, and Baubo. These appear as Old Greek epithets: *Oreobazagra*, Hecate, *Rhêichthon*. Bursting forth from the earth = Python (notably the idea of bursting forth and prophetic power exists both with Python, Typhon, and Set), *Pyripeganx* (Lord of the Font of Fire), *Hippochtôn* (= Horse-buryer, a reference to Hurrian and Greek shamanistic practices). The formula may be added to any spell that seeks to place an Idea within the body of another. The formula is MASKELLI MASKELLÔ PHÔUKENTABAO OREOBAZAGRA RHÊXICHTHÔN HIPPOCHTÔN PYRIPEGANX. This spell works by sending a message directly to the preconscious of the target, effecting his/her perceptions of pleasure and pain. The spell is charged by Necessity (Anankê). Such magic works quickly but forever changes the Fate of the magician who uses it.

Another Double Quick Action Sex Spell
PGM VII. 467-77

Take a shell from the sea and draw on it with myrrh ink the figure of Typhon given below, and in a circle write his names, and throw it into the heating chamber of a bath. But when you throw it, keep reciting these words engraved in a circle and "attract to me her, [insert name of target] whom [insert name of target's mother] bore, on this very day, from this very hour on, with her soul and heart aflame, quickly, quickly; immediately, immediately. The picture is the one below.

But when reciting the spell, say its beginning: "This is the god of Destinies," ÔKESE EERINIARE MIN ENTENTAIN PHOOU TÔNKTÔ MNE SIETHÔN OSIRI ENABÔTH PSANOU LAMPSOUÔR IEOU IÔ IÔ AI ÊI EI AI EI AÔ, attract to me her, [insert name of target], whose mother is [insert name of target's mother]," and the rest.

Notes: The papyrus omits the figure, but a donkey or Set-beast will do. These names will work:
IÔ ERBÊTH IÔ BOLCHOSÊTH IÔ PAKERBÊTH
See my advice on the last spell.

74

Love Spell
Called the Red Cloth of Nepthys
PDM lxi. 100-105

To be recited by a woman over a menstrual cloth. "Pre arose; he sent forth the *Seket* boat of heaven; the water under the bark of Pre has dried up. The gods and the two crowns (of the south and the north) complain until [insert name of target] is brought to [insert name of magician]. If not doing it is what will be done, the god whose names I said will bend down so that they fall into the fire, he will manifest for I am Nepthys, I am Shta, the future is born of me for my blood is the source of time. Khonsu obeys me and all living creatures obey me. I am the one who said it; she will repeat it 'Be destroyed, impious one!' She is the one who said it; she is the one who heard it and repeated it." It is very good when he says it.

II. Curse Tablets

Separation Tablet

This tablet was found in Athens.

Here ia a general frame-rite to be used when creating the curse tablet. Firstly, perform the frame rite from Chapter Five. Then say aloud your reasons for cursing the individual— why this operation is Needed for your self-development. Visualize your target9s). Imagine the them held in your right hand. Strike your right hand twice with your left hand, and then make the gesture of throwing your target(s) away. After this write your spell. then read it alowud. then close your rite in the manner of your choosing. Place the tablet in a suitable medium. If you want a person's anger toward you to cool— toss it in water. If you've written the spell for protectioin— lock it up somewhere safe. Experimentation and intuitiion are your guides; learning to read the signs of your world, your job.

"BÔRPHÔRBABARPHORBARBARPHORBABARPHORBABAIÊ, Oh powerful BEPTU I deliver to you Leosthenes and Peios, who frequent Juliana, to whom Marcia gave birth, so that you may chill them and their intentions, in order that they may not be able to speak or walk with one another, nor sit in Juliana's place of business, nor may Leosthenes and Peios be able to send messages to Juliana. And also chill in your gloomy air those who bring them together. Bind them in the darkened air of forgetfulness and chill and do not allow Proklos and Leosthenes

75

and Peios to have sexual/social intercourse with her. MONZOUNÊ ALCHEINÊ PERPERTHARÔNA IAIA, I deliver to you Leosthenes and Peios. Powerful Typhon KOLCHLO PONTONON Seth SACHAÔCH EA Lord APOMX PHRIOURIGX, who are in charge of disappearing and chilling, KOLCHOICHEILÔPS, may Leosthenes and Peios cool off, so that they are unable to talk with Juliana. Just as these names are cooling off, so may the names of Leosthenes and Peios cool off for Juliana and also their soul, their passion, their knowledge, their passion, their charm, their mind, their knowledge, and their reasoning. May they stand deaf, voiceless, mindless, harmless, with Juliana hearing nothing about Leosthenes and Peios and they feeling no passion or speaking with Juliana."

Notes: When composing such a tablet, use the names of the persons involved, of course. The knowledge of their Coming Into Being (i.e., their mothers' names) is a key to power over them.

The Greek magical name for Typhon is Bepon — probably influenced by the Set-cult names for Set such as Bata and BÊTH. It is a very powerful name for producing illusions of something the Magician intends to make later into reality. The "magic" of Bepon is the "magic" of the Magus.

Legal Tablet

This tablet's original location is unknown.

IAKOUB-IA IA AI BOLCHÔSÊTH IÔRBETH NEFTHYS IAÔ IAÊ IÔ-SPHÊ IÔ IÔ ABRAÔTH. Make Akeilios Phausteinos and Stephenas, my opponents in the matter concerning the slaves and concerning the personal property and concerning the papers and concerning the things of which they might accuse me, and concerning these matters may they neither think about them nor remember them; and cool off their mind, their soul, and their passion, from today and from this very hour and for the entire time of their life.

Notes: The word IÔSPHÊ is a variation of IASPHÊ, a Typhonic name also appearing as IÔSÊTH and connected linguistically with the Hebrew JOSEPH. Note that both appear side-by-side in the Galilee tablet.

Fragmentary Tablet

This tablet was found at Beth Shean in Galilee. This is provided for the names contained only.

CHUCH BACHUCH BAKACHUCH BAKAXICHUCH
BAZABACHUCH BENNEBECHUCH BADÊTOPHÔTH
BAINCHÔÔÔCH . . . ABRAZANOU SALBANACHAMBRÊ, Lord
angels, bind, bind fast the tendons and the limbs and the
thought and the mind and the intention of Sarmation, to whom
Oursa gave birth, and Valentia, to whom Eva gave birth, and
Saramannas, to whom Eusebis gave birth — muzzle them and
blind them and silence them and make them dumb . . . blind in
the presence of Pancharia to whom Thekla gave birth . . .
IÔSEPH IÔSÊTH IÔPAKERBÊTH IÔBOLCHOSÊTH IÔOSESRO IÔ
PATATHNAX IÔAPOMPS IÔTONTOLIPSKONTOLIPS IÔB...LÔBRÔ
IÔARISAXA IÔ ... IOTRI IÔDÔRUKUNXISITHIÔ IÔBOLCHOSÊTH
MÔCHIÔ IÔALO ÔSORNOPHRIX Come to me EULAMÔN Come
to me EULAMÔN ULAMÔN LAMÔN AMÔN MÔN ÔN N IÔ
Come to me EUCHALÊ IÔLEU . . . SSKUPHIELU IÔLAKÔIUATH
IÔMATHUTÔR IÔMANDOUÔR IÔCHACHACHOUÔR
IÔDARDEUB IÔPHIBITAX IÔDEDOUXATH IÔSALATH IÔSALILE
BAUI IÔCHAM IÔBACHEÔCH IÔB . . . . CH EÔOU
BAUZÔCHAIÔÔSDOUTH IÔ MASKELLI MASKELLÔ
PHNOUKENTABAÔTH OREOBARZAGRA REXICHTHÔN
HIPPONCHTHÔN PYRICHTHÔN PYRIPEGANYX LEPETAN
LEPETAN IÔBEZEBUTH IÔTHOURAKRINI BRIA BADE-
TOPHÔTH IÔDRAX IÔPHEDRA IÔARABAZA Ô
IÔIARBATHAGRA MNEPHI BLÔ CHNEMEO ARPON- KNOUPHI
BRINTATAÔPHRI BRINSKULMA A . . . CHARTH MESONKRIPHI
NIKTOU CHNOUMAÔPHI OREO- BARZAGRA KNEMEÔPHI
IÔARBATHA IÔCHTHECH . . . IA MUCHEÔ IÔPIP . . . CH . . .
ÔA . . . KANTOUNOBOETH DARDANÔ
CHITHACHÔCHENCHÔCHEÔCHI ABRASAX IÔ EUTHIN
EUTHIN, I invoke you, SEMEA KANTEU KENTEU KONTEU
KERIDEU DARUNKÔ KUKUNX KAPCHUMRE SEMESILAMPS,
Lord angels, muzzle and subject and render subservient and bind
and slave and restrain and tie up Sarmation, to whom Oursa
gave birth, and Valentia, to whom Eva gave birth, and
Saramanas, to whom Eusebis gave birth, in the presence of
Pancharia, to whom Thekla gave birth, choking them, typing up
their thoughts, their mind, their hearts, their intention, lest they
inquire further after an account or a calculation or anything else .
. . from Pancharia, but let merciful fortune come to Pancharia
throughout her life. IÔ ABLANATHANALBA IÔ
AKRAMACHAMARI IÔ SESENGEN IÔ BARPHARNGES . . .
ÔTH IÔ NEBOUTOSOUALETH AKTIÔPHI ERESCHIGAL IÔ
BERBITA IÔ THÔBAGRA BAUI . . .
ABERAMENTHÔOULERTHEXANAXETHRELUAÔTHNEMAREBA

the Great! AEMINAEBARRÔTHERRETHÔR RABAENIMEA IÔ
SARCHACHATHARIA IÔ
IAEÔBAPHRENEMOUNOTHEILARIKRIPHIAEYEAIPHIRKIRALITH
ONOU MENERPHA BÔEAI and the greatest name, PSI PSI PSI
PSI PSI K K K CH CH CH PHI PHI PHI PHI K K K CH CH . . .
I K K K K PPHIYYYDDDKKKKAKA . . . IÔSÊTH IÔ . . . BETH
IÔBOLCHOSÊTH IÔ PATATHANAX B . . . EULAMO ULAMÔE
LAMÔEU AMÔE- UL MÔEULA ÔEULAM . . . AZAZA . . . the
name of the great god IOU . . . IIIOUI . . . great . . . I invoke
you . . .

Notes: For further material on the Typhonic tradition in
Galilee, see Morton Smith's *Jesus the Magician*, a good study of
an early Typhonic magician outside of but affected by Egyptian
traditions. The name BAINCHÔÔCH means "BA" of Darkness,
the Egyptian form of Shalem, the Ugaritic god of Twilight, whose
city is Jerusalem.

To Cause Hatred

This tablet was found at Puteoli, Italy.

SEÔTHE
SABAÔTH
SABAÔTH

IAO ÊL MICHAÊL NEPHTHÔ.

the
holy
name May Gaios Stalkios Leiberarios, to whom Philista gave
birth, become an enemy of (or be hated by) Lollia Roupheina,
may he become an enemy of Haplos, may he become an enemy
of Eutuchos, may he become an enemy of Celer, may he become
an enemy of Rouphos, may he become an enemy of the entire
household of Rouphina, may he become an enemy of Polubios,
may he become an enemy of Amômis (a woman), may he
become an enemy of Thêbê. . .

Note: The spell equates the Jewish god Saboth with
Archangel Michael, the goddess Nepthys, and Set.

Protective Tablet

This tablet was found at Pontus in Asia Minor.

I am the great one who is sitting in heaven, the wandering
hollow of the cosmos ARSENONEOPHRIS, the safe name
MIARSAU as the true *daimon* BARICHAA KMEPHI who is the
ruler of the kingdoms of the gods ABRIAÔTH ALARPHÔTHO

SÊTH. Never let evil appear. Drive away, drive away the curse from Rouphina; and if someone does me an injustice, send the curse back to him. Nor let poison harm me. King of Kings ABRIAÔN TÔ ORTHIARÊ. I am the one ruling the place in Moses' name.

Notes: This protective spell is related to the magical traditions of Jeu the Hieroglyphist — who invokes the Holy Headless One first by becoming Moses then later transforming himself into a Setian deity. Jeu's name is connected with ideas of divine ascent — particularly in the *First and Second Books of Jeu* in the Bruce Codex.

Silver seems to be the metal of choice for protective spells — connected with the Moon, it gives the owner power against hazard and cyclical change.

III. From a Coptic Grimoire

Oil Spell for Sealing a Marriage with Hot Sex
Spell for mutual love between a man and a woman

Text: Michigan 4932f
Description: vellum, 5 1/2 x 15 1/4 in., "probably fairly early" (see Worrell)
Bibliography: William H. Worrell, "Coptic Magical and Medical Texts," 184-87

To be said over massage oil:

Oil! Oil! Oil! Holy oil!

Oil that flows from under the throne of Yao Sabaoth! Oil with which Isis anointed Osiris' bones! I call you, oil. The sun and moon call you. The stars of heaven call you. The servants of the sun call you. I want to send you. You must come so that I may bring you and you may bring [name of target] daughter of [name of target's mother]. to me — me, [name of magician] son of [name of magician's mother] — and you must make my love be in her heart and hers in mine like a brother and sister, or a bear who wants to suckle her young. Yea, yea, I invoke you, the one whose head is in heaven, whose feet are in the abyss, before whom is what is also under the Sheep, behind whom is what is also under Draco, the one before whom the heaven of all darkness is hung, the Holy Headless One who encircles all and who speaks to those who rise to his level in truth.

79

I shall uproot him by iron. I shall melt him away. No, my lord, do not hand me over to Dimelouchs, who judges. Instead I want you to descend to hell and uproot all thoughts of the devil about [name of target] child of [name of target's mother], and make my love be in her heart and hers in mine. For it is I who invoke: it is you who fulfill the desire.

Note: This spell appeared in a Coptic magical book. Set, he who is behind Draco, cannot be named in this Christian text. This spell appears unique in that it is designed for re-creating Love and sex in a marriage and focusing the energies of both parties *willingly* and *consciously* away from other objects of desire. A powerful spell for our age — which clearly led into the Christian tradition of anointing oils.

Here is the first example of the preconscious — the Egyptian Duat — replaced by the Greek Tartarus (Hell) — and the devil banished to this region. This spell shows Set-Sia, who fights Apep so that the right thoughts may manifest at the right time, making his last stand as the destroyer of illusion (rather than its creator). In 1966 CE he was called back. If you lack a good source of oils and incense in your area, you might try 12th House Arts & Publishing, POB 1012, Monitowoc, WI 54220. They've always done good work for me.

Chapter 7
Remanifestations and Resources

The essence of darkness reveals itself to whoever
looks at the sun.

Spell 115 of *the
Book of the Dead*

I. Remanifestations

In 1904ev in the City of Cairo a Montu priest named Ankh-f-
n-Khonsu Heard the Word of the Aeon he was to usher in, and
the Word of the Aeon which was Yet To Be. Aleister Crowley's
Word was Thelema, and the other word was "Coph" a good
XXVth dynasty pronunciation of the verb To Become. He correctly
associated the word "Coph" with the Spiral Force and the double
wands— two Egyptian symbols of sovereignty: the Set-headed
w3s scepter (pronounced WAAZ) or the scepter of Ptah, which
signifies "Dominion" — and the *Tcham* scepter (pronounced
DJAMM) which symbolizes the power to father strong children to
carry on one's work.

In addition to the auditory route of the Word, an ink trail
was forming as well. Some of the Apep books — spells that
allow the priest-magician to reach the level (*paχer*) the Apep-
slaying god had— were being published in English. The most
famous of these collections, the Bremner-Rhind papyrus, contained
a short spell which Philippe Derchain has identified as the
beginning of the Hermetic tradition. The spell in question, *The
Book* (Magical Word Gathering - djelemt) *of Knowing the Spiral
Force of Re and the Felling of Apep*, in a mysterious fashion, led
to the establishment of the Aeon of Set as well as linking the
Hermetic tradition back to the Set Priests of the New Kingdom. I
would like to examine the spell's history and meaning — and
end my scroll with a few notes on the possible resources
surrounding the current Word to aid the Magician in his task.

A Scottish lawyer Alexander H. Rhind (1833-1865) visited
Thebes at the suggestion of his doctors. The warm and dry
climate would hopefully bring Mr. Rhind a great vigor. Egypt
certainly worked its magic on him. He became involved in the
gentlemanly pursuit of archaeology as well as the wealthy man's
game of buying up the wares of the tomb robbers of Thebes.
One of his most famous acquisitions — the Egyptian Mathematical
Scroll — is our greatest window on Egypt's mathematics.

81

Mr. Rhind blossomed from his arrival in 1856 to his departure in 1863. The British Consul in Luxor, Agha Mustafa, who made a pretty penny himself in tomb robbing, arranged a going-away party for Rhind. Mustafa presented him with a scroll from the hiding place of royal mummies at Der-al-Behari, which would not be "officially" discovered (that is to say, by Europeans) for a few years yet.

"Think of it as a gift from Egypt, Mr. Rhind."

Rhind returned to England with his treasures, and began making inquiries of the British Museum. Ill-health took him even before he could have the colophon of Mustafa's papyrus translated.

The colophon dates the papyrus, identifies its owner, and curses anyone who might remove it from Egypt.

The papyrus dates from the beginning of Greek rule in Egypt. It contains ritual works: the *Songs of Isis and Nepthys, Ritual of Bringing in of Sokar,* the *Books of Overthrowing Apep* and an appendix to the last, *the Names of Apep Who Has Not Come Into Being.* Hopefully the recent (1994) find of 300 papyri of the same era at the Setian cult site of Tanis will throw further light on χeper, the eternal word of Set.

In the third section most of the Apep spells had a twofold function. Firstly, they destroyed the enemies of the Pharaoh in this world. Secondly, they provided for a *meaningful* existence in the next. Most are spells of a cruder sort — execration texts. Likewise most spells identify Apep with Set.

One spell, however, called the *Book of Knowing the Spiral Force* (Manifestation) *of Re and the Felling of Apep* dates to a much earlier source, the reign of Ramses III (1184 - 1153 BCE) — some 700 years before. This spell, containing the Divine Formula χepera χeper χeperu, is found carved on the back of a protective statue of Ramses III, the second Pharaoh of the XXth dynasty in which he is protrayed as the god χephra. This statue is at a shrine in the eastern desert where the Known lands of Khem and the Unknown lands of Desert meet. The spell allows humans to rise above their semidivine nature to the level of a god — the practice of *Paχery.* The spell may have an even earlier origin; French Egyptologist Georges Posener has suggested a Middle Kingdom origin.

The Setian significance of the spell cannot be dismissed. Ramses III's father was Setnakt, whose name means "Set is Mighty." When the chronicles of the family were written, Setnakt was described as "having the rage of the god χeper-i-Set on the battlefield." The name χeper-i-Set means "I Become Set." This is a direct reference to the practice of *Paχery* — the name χeper-i-Set being the exoteric form of the common Typhonian name *Pakerbêth*. The spell cast a different form to the then-conventional statement about a god being "self-created in all of his Forms" which had been the standard wording since the time of a Vth dynasty spell in the Pyramid Texts. There is every reason to believe that the spell belonged to the family of Set priests from whom the Pharaohs of the XIXth and XXth dynasties were descended.

I will give a magical translation of *The Book of Knowing the Spiral Force of Re and the Felling of Apep* based on R. O. Faulkner's translations of the two versions of the spell in the Bremner-Rhind papyrus (which appeared in four parts in the *Journal of Egyptian Archaeology* between 1936 and 1938), with interspersed commentary. The relationship of "I Who Have Come Into Being" and "That Which Has Come Into Being" is the law which in Late Antiquity became the "As above, so below" of the *Emerald Tablets of Hermes*. It determines the whole of Western magical practice and this is its root.

The Book of Knowing the Spiral Force of Re and the Felling of Apep

The spell achieves two functions. Firstly, it destroys delusion so that *That Which Must Be* may manifest on this earth. Secondly, it immortalizes the mind/soul complex of the reciter. Through the priest-magician transforming himself into the Lord of the Limit and then re-working the Roots of his experience — the Roots of all experience of conscious beings — are the twofold benefit of the spell Realized. It is assumed that the magician is already in possession of a Working technology of reaching the desired state.

The spell contains the fundamental Setian idea. Meaning does not come from any god or faith. Meaning derives from the essential existential fact of knowledge of Self-Being. The strata of seeming meaning which prevents the Real from manifesting in the world is the snake Apep, "he of the broken kas". Apep is a semi-sentient entity formed from dreams which have not manifested. Apep is said to be a "magician" whose spells are not in accordance with his mind.

The Lord of the Limit says

This unnamed god is the god of the limit of Consciousness — all of Self versus non-Self. By speaking, it is transformed by willed memory into the Principle of Isolate Intelligence.

83

I have Come Into Being and by my Coming Into Being the way of Coming Into Being Came Into Being.

This is the Divine Formula of *χepera χeper χeperu*.

𓆣𓏤𓆣𓆣𓏌

It is the seed of the whole spell and establishes the relationship between interior and exterior existence, Thought and Action, and the propagation of Will throughout the world. It is the basis of all Setian magic. When Wallis Budge wrote his *Egyptian Language: Easy Lessons in Egyptian Hieroglyphics* (1910 Kegan Paul, reprinted 1966) he chose the Divine Formula for one of his grammar exercises. Michael Aquino purchased a copy of the book circa 1970 to spice up the rituals of the Church of Satan Grotto he led — the Chaldean Grotto of Louisville, Kentucky. Although he thought the phrase novel, he attributed no special significance to it — nor was he aware of its origin from *The Book of Knowing the Spiral Force of Re and the Felling of Apep*. Significantly, there were some signs of its influence which can be seen in two of the sections he wrote for *The Satanic Rituals*, "The Ceremony of the Nine Angles" and "The Adult Satanic Baptism." His magical name at the time was Marduk, a figure who slays Tiamat, much in the manner of Set's slaying Apep.

In 1975 a series of crises in the Church of Satan, which on a magical level involved the breaking down of the Self barriers of its Magus, caused Michael Aquino to invoke the Prince of Darkness in Need. The results of that Working were a magical communication called *The Book of Coming Forth by Night*. Its title is a clear reference to the Osirian Book of the Dead, *The Book of Coming Forth by Day*. In the *Book of Coming Forth by Night*, Set reveals his Word of *χeper*. The effect of the *Book* was to fell a delusional system and Create an Initiatory school whose Secret of exuding Being will prove to be fundamental in the Shaping of liberated humanity. This statement of self-isolation, self-creation, and self-manifestation is the sublime counterpart to the operative isolative spells of the magical papyri.

The word *χeper* was oddly not investigated during the nineteen years following the founding of the Temple — it became a mystery reserved for the next Magus of the Word. With each individual's discovery and application of the psychic realization of "I have Come into Being" the influence on the world (i.e., the number of Walls which suddenly Become Doors) increases. This idea — as in the time of the magical papyri — is the key to the magical Will.

I Came Into Being in the shape of χepera, who
Came Into Being on the First Occasion. I Came Into
Being in the shape of χepera, and that is how "Being"
Came Into Being. I was the First Cause of First Causes
and my name was more primeval than the primeval
ones I made.

This is a restatement of the Divine Law. It has three notable
ideas. Firstly, that the moment of Self-realization is one of self-
shaping — that the stuff of consciousness is organized into a
right-brain pattern — and that this *shape* is not consciousness
itself but a begetter of further shapes. A reflection of this process
occurs every time one becomes aware of one's own Being — or
every time one calls a meeting to order. Secondly, the shape
gives way to a Name — a left-brain process that orders all other
concepts. (These two ideas are bound up in the Egyptian term for
hieroglyphs *Medu Neter* — "messengers of the god".) Thirdly,
the Name is not revealed, indicating that this is not a spell for
achieving union/identification with a particular god, but for
entering the divine realm itself at the highest level of activity.

I did all I desired in this land and pervaded all of
it.
The phrase "I did all I desired" is found in the various after-
death spells indicating the liberated state of the psyche in its
timeless form free from the limits of the five senses and four
dimensions. The spell both taps into the state so that power may
be brought from that Unmanifest region to the Earth — and
helps the postmodern psyche to remember its limits of self-
definition so that the Apep serpent won't devour it.

Being Alone I knit my own hand before I made
Shu or spat Tefnut. I used my mouth and "Magic" was
my Name. It was I who Came Into Being in my shape.
I Came Into Being and there Came Into Being a
number of primeval ones. I alone achieved this. There
was none who could act in my place. I alone achieved
this in my soul; I created some of them in Nun as
Inert Ones, when I could as yet find no place to
stand. I considered my Mind, I surveyed with my
sight and I alone achieved all that was made; I
planned in my Mind I created another being, and
manifold were the Shapes of χepera; their Children
Came Into Being after the manner of those Shapes.

85

The words for "primeval" in the section above present almost as great a piece of wordplay as the many plays on the word χeper. They are various forms of *Paa*. *Paa* is a magical first occasion, a self-contained circle that the future pirials out from, that is to say, the Unmanifest. It contains all potentials in a static form.

The first action in this first cycle of creation is the creation of a hand, both for manipulating and autoerotic purposes. Touch is the third internal or subjective sense, created after Vision (Will) and Hearing (Understanding).

The next action is a Self-Naming through Doing. The Nameless One becomes Heka, the god of Magic — of the Imaging principle. With the coming of Magic ends the First Cycle of Creation: a number of formal prerequisites — the categories of thought — are created. These are proto-gods of duality. All of this was achieved in the subjective universe of the Unnamed One.

The Second Cycle of Creation begins with the creation of the unchanging laws of the Objective Universe. These are the Inert Ones in Nun. With an observable universe, a Mind can be fashioned, because an external consistent universe is the grain against which a semi-constant internal universe is formed. This ends the Second Cycle of Creation.

The Third Cycle of Creation begins with the Unnamed One considering his Mind. This place of psychic order (or Ma'at) Becomes a funneling mechanism for the Chaos of Thought. Through the interaction of Mind and Thought, the Unnamed One creates another Being. This other Being is unnamed but is the god or goddess of phenomenological randomness. Just as the First held in itSelf all Being, all Becoming in its many forms reside in this other. Both are ultimately One — the two faces of Being and Becoming connected and Hidden in the word χeper. This oneness permits communication and *resonance* between different entities now. Both faces partake of χeper and thus can communicate and interact at a higher level of Being than might be expected from their descent from the Principle of Isolate Intelligence. This mystery allows the magic of the Aeon of Set to work — and an Understanding and *enactment* of this Mystery from the simplest act of sorcery to the actions of a philosopher-king is the property that allows for evolution and remanifestations of the self.

The Mystery explains *how* magic works and in what areas magic is most likely to work. This ends the Third Cycle of Creation.

It was I who spat out Shu and expectorated Tefnut.
I aroused myself with my hand and swallowing my
own seed spat it forth again as Shu and Tefnut. They
went beyond me into Nun where they rejoiced. I who
had Come Into Being alone now knew of three other
gods. I waited for two eternities for Shu and Tefnut to
return to me.

The way to create gods in the Objective Universe (i.e., in
Nun) is an autoerotic procedure. The significance of this is that
such created gods are *not* the same type of entity as the forms
created by Mind alone. They partake of the *essential* patterns that
the Creator went through in his own self-creation — but are
themselves subject to the dynamic nature of evolution. These two
entities Shu and Tefnut represent intellect and emotion, male and
female, dividing and joining. Shu separates the past (*djet*) from
the future (*neheh*), the subjective from the objective. Tefnut joins
all of these things. These beings *rejoiced* in Nun because their
powers of understanding are more appropriate to the objective
outer realm. They represent the *force* of understanding which in
addition to Being is one of the ways the psyche effects Nun.
Notably these beings did not return to the unnamed god without
the named god coercing them! This represents the long period of
life without initiation while the process of reason and emotion
cause the body-soul complex to accumulate enough data for the
initiatory process. (These two gods may be invoked by the
magician under the name of Shuti [Shu-Tefnut] or Routi
[Yesterday-Tomorrow]).

Nun brought them up. I made an Eye and sent
after them. My Eye brought them back to me and I
united myself. I wept over the whole of my being and
from my tears did mankind Come Into Being. My Eye
was angered that I had grown another Eye in its
absence. I pulled my second Eye from my face and
made it the arranger of destiny.

By observing, interacting, altering, and playing with the
watery Chaos of the world, Shu and Tefnut are educated. The
Magician is not raised by his family or circumstance to be a
Magician — nor is circumstance sufficient to awaken him to his
or her true state of existence. Another force proceeding from the
unnamed god in the form of the Sun returns them to a dark
place lit by the moon. There the unnamed god unites its internal

faces of Being and Becoming with Reason and Emotion — from this crucial enactment of understanding — a holy tearful moment — are born all of the many men and women whom the Magician may have to be, or work through, as his Essence flows forth in a multiplicity of manifestations. Shu is the application of critical thinking. It is willed skeptical rationality that dissects external events. Tefnut, goddess of joy (*tefen*) is the integrative wholeness that comes from the feeling of resistance being overcome. From the integrative moment χ*eper* (Becoming) is cast into the world, Shu and Tefnut are re-united, and the sun and moon made. This moment of Union with Shu and Tefnut (who themselves are one god/goddess Shuti) is the root of alchemical dialectic *solve et coagula*. The sun symbolized by the constant commandment to Seek is angered by the Changing moon, who constantly hides and creates illusion by changing light. Yet the moon is given the power to arrange destiny. The unnamed god is left in darkness.

And Shu and Tefnut begat Geb and Nuit and Geb and Nuit begat in one birth Osiris, Horus the blinded, Set, Isis and Nepthys and they begat and begat and created many children on Earth and are linked to children bearing their Forms.

The begetting of Earth and Sky and their five children brings the level of manifestation to the day-to-day objective world. The epithet of Horus indicates the Setian nature of the text — this is the elder Horus, Set's brother not his nephew. Notably all of mankind has a dual heritage — one from the unnamed god and the other from one or more of the five gods of the world. The first reflects the great hidden potential for Becoming that lies within each human breast — the other is a combination of psychological makeups. We may all partake of all five, but only those of a strong descent of one or the other may be *energized* by performing magical actions by someone risen up (*pa*χ*er*) in the Name of the god or goddess who is their primary ancestor.

They made conjuration that they might fell their foes. They created magic spells for felling Apep. He is imprisoned in the arms of Aker, he has neither arms nor legs, and is bound in one place, according to Re who obstructs him, for Re has commanded that he be felled on account of his evil character. Children fell him and sunder his soul from his shade — he is

despoiled and there will be no portion for him in the
Land of Desire. Those in the North, in the West, in
the South, and in the East have felled him.

This is the operative portion of the Book — a statement that
keeps the force of delusion at bay — it is the fierce battle for
existence and *extension of existence* against those forces of
madness, sadness, and despair that could end the manifestation of
Isolate Intelligence in the universe. Each of the patterns has a
way of fighting he who does not exist: Osiris by resting beneath
the ground, Horus by cooperative warfare, Set by active extension
of existence through Initiation, Isis by nurturing and pulling
living patterns from the past, Nepthys by resonance with future
selves. Lastly the forces of mankind are invoked counter-clockwise
(indicating again the Setian/Polar bias of the spell versus the
clockwise solar order).

O you sages on Earth and you Nine Gods who
came into Being from my flesh, be vigilant in felling
Apep. Exorcise him and destroy his name, do not
permit his name to be spread abroad; his children
shall not exist, his seat shall not exist, and he shall
have neither soul nor body nor spirit, for he belongs
to the Eye of Re, and it has power over him and it
devours him. I am he who has committed Apep to the
Flame. I have allotted him to the heat, I have given
him over to the Eye of Re which has parched him. It
has consumed his body, soul, spirit, shade, and magic.
He shall neither copulate nor become erect forever.

Delusion — any imprecise fanciful knowledge that leads
towards dissolution rather than transformation — is to be fought
by Sages (i.e., humans possessed of Lore) and the Nine Gods.
Nine is the traditional number of gods in the barque of Re. They
represent the ruling principles which govern the Cosmos. It is the
way of the Setian Hermeticist to have those principles living in
him — not be calling down some entity from elsewhere, but by
Creating them as semi-constant patterns (raised from and
connected to the subconscious) — that serve and protect the core
self, that which has Come Into Being. A good "set" of nine for
the Typhonian magician are χepera, Ma'at, Shuti, Geb, Nuit,
Osiris, Set, Isis, and Nepthys.
   The actions against Apep begin with exorcising him (that is,
using spells against those persons or events which stand against

That Which Must Be), then destroying his Name — uprooting the paths to delusional thinking in your own mind. Then being sure that his name is not spread abroad — this is the commitment to stand against hypocrisy and the command to remove any bad ideas you yourself have put in the world, even if it embarrasses you to do so.

Likewise the Children of Apep are to be banished and his seat destroyed. He is committed to the flames — to the Eye of Re. That constant command, to bring reason and emotion back to the source, is the force which destroys Apep.

The sun, which brings periodic unity of the self in service to the dark unnamed god, destroys Apep and provides an eternal vision of the Real.

This short spell is a technology for accessing the innermost fact of Being and then using the *gnosis* gained thereby to destroy illusion, delusion, and hindrance in the world. It is a spell of both Inspiration and Transformation. It brought the potential of Setian Initiation from the Second Blooming to the Third — and its core form of χepera χeper χeperu opened the Door afresh in 1975.

The Setian Hermeticist will wish to consider the implications of a religious technology that gives each individual access to power and knowledge — rather than the religions of the Book which shape others based on the visions of men long dead. With this spell the flood of the Future begins anew!

II. Resources

I will give some remarks on the Internet, present a suggested reading list, and discuss the Temple of Set.

Because of the quick turnover in on-line services I won't list any electronic addresses. However, the Oriental Institute of Chicago and the British Museum both have WWW pages. There are scholarly lists on Egyptian and Ancient Near East topics. In the rapidly foreseeable future we will have access to every piece of scholarship in the world. The postmodern magician *needs* to become computer literate. He or she needs to learn how to browse the Web.

The World Wide Web is the latest remanifestation of the *per Ankh of Setne Khamuast.*

III. A Few Titles for Your Library

Flowers, Stephen E., ed. *Hermetic Magic: The Postmodern Magical Papyrus of Abaris.* York Beach, ME: Samuel Weiser, 1995.

[This book is *essential* to the practice. It places a strong emphasis on Hellenic aspects of practice as well as providing data on the meaning of names in the spells. A must-have.]

Betz, Hans Dieter, ed. *The Greek Magical Papyri in Translation Including the Demotic Spells*. Vol. 1, *Texts*. Chicago: University of Chicago Press, 1992. 2nd ed.

[The scholarly compendium of translations, this is where serious practitioners will go after this little book.]

Gager, John G., ed. *Curse Tablets and Binding Spells from the Ancient World*. New York: Oxford University Press, 1992.

[The scholarly compendium of translations of the curse tablets. See remarks above.]

Faraone, Christopher A. and Dirk Obbink, eds. *Magika Hiera: Ancient Greek Magic & Religion*. New York: Oxford University Press, 1991.

[A collection of thoughtful essays on the nature of magical practice in its cultural setting. It needs to be read with the following book.]

Bagnall, Roger S. *Egypt in Late Antiquity*. Princeton, NJ: Princeton University Press, 1993.

[This is a very good introduction to the social and political concerns of Late Antique Egypt.]

Ritner, Robert Kriech. *The Mechanics of Ancient Egyptian Magical Practice*. Studies in Ancient Oriental Civilization, No. 54. Chicago, IL: Oriental Institute of the University of Chicago, 1993.

[This is the single best source of accurate data on Egyptian magical practice.]

te Velde, H. *Seth, God of Confusion: A Study of His Role in Egyptian Mythology and Religion*. Leiden: E. J. Brill, 1977. Corrected ed.

[The only full-length study of the complexities of the god Set. Te Velde focuses on Set in pre-dynastic and dynastic times. The information here provides a precise map of the way the human psyche manifests and reacts to the manifestation of the Principle of Isolate Intelligence.]

Hornung, Eric. *Idea into Image: Essays on Ancient Egyptian Thought*. Trans. by Elizabeth Bredeck. N. p.: Timken Publishers, 1992.

[One of the best and easiest to read introductions to Egyptian thought. Particularly useful for Egyptian time concepts.]

Wilkinson, Richard H. *Symbol & Magic in Egyptian Art*. New York: Thames and Hudson, 1994.

[A beautiful book which will teach aesthetics and the importance of the visual in Egyptian magic. Chapters on hieroglyphs, actions, gestures, colors, and numbers make this an essential guide for the working magician or artist. The Egyptians themselves sometimes equated magic (*heka*) with artistic creativity.]

Richardson, Alan and B. Walker-John. *The Inner Guide to Egypt*. Bath, UK: Arcania Press, 1991.

[Although the Egyptology is dated, this presents a very good training in visualization for the beginning magician. Don't read it; *Work* your way through it.]

Brier, Bob. *Ancient Egyptian Magic*. New York: Quill, 1981.

[Good overview for the beginner, useful selection of spells — all written in a fun and easy-to-read style.]

Valantasis, Richard. *Spiritual Guides of the Third Century: A Semiotic Study of the Guide-Disciple Relationship in Christianity, Neoplatonism, Hermetism, and Gnosticism*. Harvard Dissertations in Religion No. 27. Minneapolis, MN: Fortress Press, 1991.

[An *essential* book on the role of the Teacher in magical training. This book is a must for those who would Open their own Mouths. The texts covered are representative of Christianity, Neoplatonism, Hermeticism, and Gnosticism.]

Fowden, Garth. *The Egyptian Hermes: A Historical Approach to the Late Pagan Mind*. Mythos Series. Princeton, NJ: Princeton University Press, 1993.

[A very good study of the figure of Hermes. This book is recommended for any who are serious at tackling Betz for their own initiatory and magical purposes.]

Bonnefoy, Yves, ed. *Greek and Egyptian Mythologies*. Trans. by Wendy Doninger. Chicago: University of Chicago Press, 1991.

[Of particular use to the understanding of the magician are Philippe Derchain's essays on Egyptian soulcraft and the Divine; Erik Iverson's essay "On the Fate of the Egyptian Gods," which is vital for the European magician seeking to trace the powerful effect of Hermeticism through his or her own culture; J. Leclant's essay "Meroitic Religion," which is useful for the African magician tracing the influence of Egypt in both African and Indian magic; and the essays on Plato and Neoplatonic thinking. This book will not serve as a dictionary or quick reference — the best quick reference for Egyptian gods and goddesses is George Hart's *A Dictionary of Egyptian Gods and Goddesses* (London: Routledge & Kegan Paul, 1986) which is affordable and up to date.]

These are a very bare beginning. Pursuing them will lead you to other Doors.

Lastly I'll mention the Temple of Set. It provides a focus for Initiates who wish to pursue self-deification through the practice of an antinomian magical initiatory system. It makes strong demands on its initiates in terms of intellect, magical ability, philosophical sensitivity, and real world power.

There are many studies within the Temple, of which magical Egyptology is an important one. However, the Temple has many interests, from vampyres to Runic studies, from political science to the magical uses of man's most modern technologies, and is ever hoping to discover new fields to aid in the process of Self-deification. If you have had success with your magic, if you are dedicated and strong of will, you might consider writing to the TOS at Post Office Box 470307; San Francisco, CA 94147; U.S.A.

The Fire has been called down from Heaven, the AH3U SUTK persists upon the Earth.

February 14, 1996ev
Austin, Texas - San Francisco

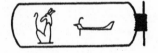

Bibliography

Aldred, Cyril. *Egypt to the End of the Old Kingdom*. Library of the Early Civilizations. Ed. by Stuart Piggott. New York: McGraw-Hill Book Company, 1965.

Andrews, Carol. *Amulets of Ancient Egypt*. Austin: University of Texas Press, 1994.

Aquino, Michael. "Black Magic" in *The Crystal Tablet of Set*. San Francisco: The Temple of Set, 1993 and various earlier dates.

Aquino, Michael. *Book of Coming Forth by Night*. In *The Ruby Tablet of Set*. San Francisco: The Temple of Set, 1975.

Baal, J. van. *Symbols for Communication: An Introduction to the Anthropological Study of Religion*. Studies of Developing Countries. Assen: Van Gorrcum, 1971.

Badawy, Alexander. *Ancient Egyptian Architectural Design: A Study of the Harmonic System*. Berkeley and Los Angeles: University of California Press, 1965.

Bagnall, Roger S. *Egypt in Late Antiquity*. Princeton, NJ: Princeton University Press, 1993.

Bell, H. Idris. *Cults and Creeds in Graeco-Roman Egypt*. Chicago: Ares Publishers, 1957.

Berchman, Robert M. "Arcana Mundi: Prophecy and Divination in the Vita Mosis of Philo of Alexandria" in *The Ancient World Mystery Cults in Late Antiquity*, Vol XXVI, Num. 2, 1995, pp. 150-179.

Betz, Hans Dieter, ed. *The Greek Magical Papyri in Translation Including the Demotic Spells*. Vol. 1, *Texts*. Chicago: University of Chicago Press, 1992. 2nd ed.

Boas, George, trans. *The Hieroglyphics of Horapollo*. Bollingen Series XXIII. Princeton, NJ: Princeton University Press, 1950. Mythos Books ed., 1993.

Bonnefoy, Yves, ed. *American, African, and Old European Mythologies*. Trans. by Wendy Doninger. Chicago: University of Chicago Press, 1992.

Bonnefoy, Yves, ed. *Greek and Egyptian Mythologies*. Trans. by Wendy Doninger. Chicago: University of Chicago Press, 1991.

Bottero, Jean. *Mesopotamia: Writing, Reasoning, and the Gods*. Trans. by Zainab Bahrani and Marc vad de Mieroop. Chicago: University of Chicago Press, 1992.

Bowman, Alan K. *Egypt after the Pharaohs: 332BC-AD642 from Alexander to the Arab Conquest.* Berkeley and Los Angeles: University of California Press, 1989.

Boylan, Patrick. *Thoth: The Hermes of Egypt.* London: n.p., 1922. Reprinted Chicago: Ares Publications, 1987.

Breasted, James Henry. *A History of Egypt: From the Earliest Times to the Persian Conquest.* New York: Charles Scribner's Sons, 1909. 2d ed. Hudson River ed.

Bremmer, Jan N. *The Early Greek Concept of the Soul.* Princeton, NJ: Princeton University Press, 1983. Mythos edition.

Brier, Bob. *Ancient Egyptian Magic.* New York: Quill, 1981.

Buchanan, James J., and Harold T. Davis. *Zosimus: Historia Nova: The Decline of Rome.* San Antonio, TX: Trinity University Press, 1967.

Budge, E. A. Wallis. *Amulets and Talismans.* Originally *Amulets and Superstitions.* Oxford: n.p., 1930. Reprinted New York: Collier Books, 1970.

Budge, E. A. Wallis. *The Bandlet of Righteousness: An Ethiopian Book of the Dead.* Reprinted Edmonds, WA: Near Eastern Press, 1985.

Budge, E. A. Wallis. *The Egyptian Book of the Dead: The Papyrus of Ani in the British Museum. The Egyptian Text with Interlinear Transliteration and Translation, a Running Translation, Introduction, Etc.* London: n.p., 1895. Reprinted New York: Dover Publications, 1967.

Budge, E. A. Wallis. *Egyptian Language: Easy Lessons in Egyptian Hieroglyphics.* London: Kegan Paul, 1910 and 1966. Reprinted New York: Dover Publications, 1983.

Budge, E. A. Wallis. *Egyptian Magic.* Originally *Books of Egypt and Chaldea,* Vol. 2. London: Kegan Paul, 1901. Reprinted New York: Dover Publications, 1971.

Budge, E. A. Wallis. *The Liturgy of Funerary Offerings: The Egyptian Texts with English Translations.* London: Kegan Paul, 1909. Reprinted New York: Dover Publications, 1994.

Burkert, Walter. *Ancient Mystery Cults.* Cambridge, MA: Harvard University Press, 1987.

Butler, E. M. *The Myth of the Magus.* Cambridge: Cambridge University Press, 1948. Canto ed. 1993.

Cagliostro's Secret Ritual of Egyptian Rite Freemasonry. Kila, MT: Kessinger Publishers, n.d. of reprint edition.

Canfora, Luciano. *The Vanished Library: A Wonder of the Ancient World*. Trans. by Martin Ryle. Berkeley and Los Angeles: University of California Press, 1990. Corrected trans.

Clayton, Peter. *Chronicles of the Pharaohs: The Reign-by-Reign Record of the Rulers and Dynasties of Ancient Egypt*. London: Thames and Hudson, 1994.

Corbin, Henry. *Creative Imagination in the Sufism of Ibn 'Arabi*. Trans. by Ralph Manheim. Bollingen Series XCI. Princeton, NJ: Princeton University Press, 1981.

Davidson, Basil. *The African Genius: An Introduction to African Social and Cultural History*. Boston: Little, Brown and Company, 1969.

Davies, W. V. *Egyptian Hieroglyphics*. Berkeley and Los Angeles: University of California Press, 1987.

The Divine Pymander of Hermes Mercurius Trismegistus. Trans. by Dr. Everard (1650). Madras, India: n.p., 1884.

Doresse, Jean. *The Secret Books of the Egyptian Gnostics: An Introduction to the Gnostic Coptic manuscripts discovered at Chenoboskion*. Rochester, VT: Inner Traditions International, 1986.

Drower, E. S. *A Mandean Book of Black Magic*. Edmonds, WA: Alexandrian Press, 1990.

DuQuesne, Terence. *Anubis and the Spirits of the West*. Oxfordshire Communications in Egyptology 1. Thame Oxon, UK: Darengo Publications, 1990.

DuQuesne, Terence. *Caduceus: New Poems and Translations*. Miami Beach, FL: The Yeats Club, 1989.

DuQuesne, Terence. *Jackal at the Shaman's Gate: A Study of Anubis Lord of Ro-Setawe*. Oxfordshire Communications in Egyptology 3. Thame Oxon, UK: Darengo Publications, 1991.

Edwards, Amelia B. *Egypt and its Monuments: Pharaohs, Fellahas and Explorers*. New York: Harper & Brothers, 1891.

Edwards, I. E. S. *The Pyramids of Egypt*. New York: Penguin Books, 1967. Revised ed.

Egyptian Mysteries: An Account of an Initiation. York Beach, ME: Samuel Weiser, 1988.

Elgood, P. G. *Later Dynasties of Egypt*. Oxford: Basil Blackwell, 1951.

Emery, W. B. *Archaic Egypt*. Baltimore, MD: Penguin Books, 1961.

Evola, Julius. *Eros and the Mysteries of Love: The Metaphysics of Sex*. Rochester, VT: Inner Traditions International, 1983.

Faraone, Christopher A., and Dirk Obbink, eds. *Magika Hiera: Ancient Greek Magic & Religion*. New York: Oxford University Press, 1991.

Faulkner, Raymond O. *A Concise Dictionary of Middle Egyptian*. Oxford: Griffith Institute, 1991.

Faulkner, Raymond O. "The Papyrus Bremner-Rhind", published in 4 parts in *Journal of Egyptian Archaeology* 22, 1936, pp. 121-140; *JEA* 23, 1937, pp. 10-16 and pp. 166-185; and *JEA* 24, 1938, pp. 41-53.

Filoramo, Giovanni. *A History of Gnosticism*. Trans. by Anthony Alcock. Cambridge, MA: Blackwell, 1990.

Flowers, Stephen E., ed. *Hermetic Magic: The Postmodern Magical Papyrus of Abaris*. York Beach, ME: Samuel Weiser, 1995.

Flowers, Stephen E. *Lords of the Left-Hand Path: A History of Spiritual Dissent*. Smithville, TX: Rûna-Raven, [forthcoming].

Fobes, Francis H. *Philosophical Greek: An Introduction*. Chicago: University of Chicago Press, 1957.

Fontenrose, Joseph. *Python: A Study of Delphic Myth and Its Origins*. Berkeley and Los Angeles: University of California Press, 1980. California Library reprint ed.

Fowden, Garth. *The Egyptian Hermes: A Historical Approach to the Late Pagan Mind*. Mythos Series. Princeton, NJ: Princeton University Press, 1993.

Fox, Robin Lane. *The Unauthorized Version: Truth and Fiction in the Bible*. New York: Vintage Books, 1993.

Frankfort, Henri. *Ancient Egyptian Religion: An Interpretation*. New York: Harper & Row, 1948. Harper Torchbook ed. 1961.

Gager, John G., ed. *Curse Tablets and Binding Spells from the Ancient World*. New York: Oxford University Press, 1992.

Gardiner, Alan. *Egypt of the Pharaohs: An Introduction*. London: Oxford University Press, 1961.

Garin, Eugenio. *Astrology in the Renaissance: The Zodiac of Life*. London: Arkana, 1990.

Godwin, Joscelyn. *The Mystery of the Seven Vowels in Theory and Practice*. Grand Rapids, MI: Phanes Press, 1991.

Goodenough, Erwin R. *Jewish Symbols in the Greco-Roman Period*. Jacob Neusner, ed. Bollingen Series. Princeton, NJ: Princeton University Press, 1988. Abridged ed.

Goodwin, Charles Wycliffe, trans. *Fragment of a Graeco-Egyptian Work Upon Magic from a Papyrus in the British Museum*. N.p.: Cthonios Books, n.d.

Grant, Michael. *Atlas of Ancient History, 1700 BC to 565 AD*. N.p.: Dorset Press, 1983.

Gray, John. *Near Eastern Mythology: Mesopotamia, Syria, Palestine*. London: Hamlyn Publishing Group, 1969.

Griffith, F. L., and Herbert Thompson, eds. *The Leyden Papyrus: An Egyptian Magical Book*. Originally *The Demotic Magical Papyri of London and Leiden*. 1904. Reprinted New York: Dover Publications, 1974.

Hart, George. *A Dictionary of Egyptian Gods and Goddesses*. London: Routledge & Kegan Paul, 1986.

Hart, George. *Egyptian Myths*. The Legendary Past series. Austin: University of Texas Press, 1990.

Hesiod: Theogony, Works and Days, Shield. Trans. by Apostolos N. Athanassakis. Baltimore: Johns Hopkins University Press, 1983.

Hobbs, Joseph J. *Bedouin Life in the Egyptian Wilderness*. Austin: University of Texas Press, 1989.

Hoch, James E. *Middle Egyptian Grammar*. Toronto: SSEA, 1995. Forthcoming.

Hook, S. H. *Middle Eastern Mythology*. New York: Penguin Books, 1963.

Hornung, Eric. *Conceptions of God in Ancient Egypt: The One and the Many*. Trans. by John Baines. Ithaca, NY: Cornell University Press, 1982.

Hornung, Eric. *Idea into Image: Essays on Ancient Egyptian Thought*. Trans. by Elizabeth Bredeck. N. p.: Timken Publishers, 1992.

Hornung, Eric. *The Tomb of Pharaoh Seti I*. Zurich: Artemis Verlag, 1991.

Hurry, Jamieson B. *Imhotep: The Egyptian God of Medicine*. Oxford: n.p., 1926. Reprinted Chicago: Ares Publications, 1987.

Iversen, Erik. *The Myth of Egypt and Its Hieroglyphs in European Tradition*. Princeton, NJ: Princeton University Press, 1961. Mythos edition, 1993.

Jacq, Christian. *Egyptian Magic*. Trans. by Janet M. Davis. Chicago: Bolchazy-Carducci Publishers, 1985.

Jenkins, Nancy. *The Boat Beneath the Pyramid: King Cheops'
   Royal Ship*. New York: Holt, Rinehart and Winston,
   1980.
Johnson, Janet H., ed. *Life in a Multi-Cultural Society: Egypt
   from Cambyses to Constantine and Beyond*. Studies in
   Ancient Oriental Civilization, No. 51. Chicago: Oriental
   Institute of the University of Chicago, 1992.
Johnson, Janet H. *Thus Wrote 'Onchsheshonqy: An
   Introductory Grammar of Demotic*. Studies in Ancient
   Oriental Civilization, No. 45. Chicago: Oriental Institute
   of the University of Chicago, 1986. 2d ed., revised 1991.
Jonas, Hans. *The Gnostic Religion: The Message of the Alien
   God and the Beginnings of Christianity*. Boston: Beacon
   Press, 1958. 2nd ed, enlarged 1963.
Kees, Hermann. *Ancient Egypt: A Cultural Topography*. Ed.
   by T. G. H. James and trans. by Ian F. D. Morrow.
   Chicago: University of Chicago Press, 1961. Phoenix
   edition, 1977.
Keuls, Eva. *The Water Carriers in Hades: A Study of
   Catharsis through Toil in Classical Antiquity*.
   Amsterdam: Adolf M. Hakkert Publisher, 1974.
King, Francis. *Magic: The Western Tradition*. London: Thames
   and Hudson, 1975.
Klein, Ernest. *Etymological Dictionary of the Hebrew
   Language for Readers of English*. New York: Macmillon
   Publishing Company, 1987.
Klimkeit, Hans Joachim, trans. *Gnosis on the Silk Road:
   Gnostic Texts from Central Asia*. San Francisco:
   HarperSanFrancisco, 1993.
Kramer, Samuel Noah. *The Sumerians: Their History, Culture,
   and Character*. Chicago: University of Chicago Press,
   1963.
Krupp, E. C. *Echoes of the Ancient Skies: The Astronomy of
   Lost Civilizations*. New York: Harper & Row,
   Publishers, 1983.
Lamplugh, F. *The Gnosis of the Light: A Translation of the
   Untitled Apocalypse Contained in the Codex Brucianus
   (1918)*. Kila, MT: Kessinger Publishers, n.d. of reprint
   edition.
LaVey, Anton Szandor. *The Satanic Rituals*. Secaucus, NJ:
   University Books, 1972.
Leland, Charles Godfrey. *Etruscan Magic & Occult Remedies*.
   New Hyde Park, NY: University Press, 1963.

A Lexicon: Abridged from Liddell and Scott's Greek-English Lexicon. Oxford: Oxford University Press, 1976.

Lichtheim, Miriam. *Ancient Egyptian Literature: Vol. 1: The Old and Middle Kingdoms.* Berkeley and Los Angeles: University of California Press, 1975.

Lichtheim, Miriam. *Ancient Egyptian Literature: Vol. 2: The New Kingdom.* Berkeley and Los Angeles: University of California Press, 1976.

Lichtheim, Miriam. *Ancient Egyptian Literature: Vol. 3: The Late Period.* Berkeley and Los Angeles: University of California Press, 1980.

Lovecraft, H. P. *Miscellaneous Writings.* Ed. by S. T. Joshi. Sauk City, WI: Arkham House Publishers, 1995.

Loyd, S., and H. W. Müller. *Ancient Architecture.* History of World Architecture series. New York: Rizzoli International Publishers, 1982. Revised paperback ed.

Luck, Georg. *Arcana Mundi: Magic and the Occult in the Greek and Roman Worlds.* Baltimore: John Hopkins University Press, 1985.

McCall, Henrietta. *Mesopotamian Myths.* The Legendary Past series. Austin: University of Texas Press, 1990.

Malandra, William M., trans. *An Introduction to Ancient Iranian Religion: Readings from the Avesta and the Achaemenid Inscriptions.* Minneapolis, MN: University of Minnesota Press, 1983.

Manniche, Lise. *City of the Dead: Thebes in Egypt.* Chicago: University of Chicago Press, 1987.

Manniche, Lise. *Music and Musicians in Ancient Egypt.* London: British Museum Press, 1991.

Mead, G. R. S. *Fragments of a Faith Forgotten: The Gnostics: A Contribution to the Study of the Origins of Christianity.* New Hyde Park, NY: University Books, 1960.

Mead, G. R. S. *The Hymns of Hermes.* Grand Rapids, MI: Phanes Press, 1991.

Mercer, Samuel A. B. *The Pyramid Texts in Translation and Commentary.* 4 Vol. New York: Longmans, Green and Co., 1952.

Mertz, Barbara. *Temples, Tombs, and Hieroglyphs: The Story of Egyptology.* New York: Dell Publishing, 1964.

Meyer, Marvin, and Richard Smith, eds. *Ancient Christian Magic: Coptic Texts of Ritual Power.* New York: HarperSanFrancisco, 1994.

Moldenke, Charles E., ed. *The Tale of the Two Brothers: A Fairy Tale of Ancient Egypt.* First published 1892. Baltimore, MD: Black Classic Press, 1988 reprint ed.

Neugebauer, O. *The Exact Sciences in Antiquity.* New York: Barnes & Noble Books, 1993. 2d ed.

Nou, Jean-Louis, ed. *Proud Horses, Proud Riders.* New York: Tabard Press, 1986. English ed. 1989.

Pagels, Elaine. *Adam, Eve, and the Serpent.* New York: Random House, 1988.

Pagels, Elaine. *The Gnostic Gospels.* New York: Vintage Books, 1981.

Pennick, Nigel. *Secret Games of the Gods: Ancient Ritual Systems in Board Games.* London: Kegan Paul, 1989. Reprinted York Beach, ME: Samuel Weiser, 1989.

Pinch, Geraldine. *Magic in Ancient Egypt.* Austin: University of Texas Press, 1995.

Plotinus, *The Enneads.* Trans. by Stephen MacKenna. London: Penguin Books, 1991. Abridged ed.

Porphyry's Against the Christians: *The Literary Remains.* Trans. by R. Joseph Hoffmann. Amherst, NY: Prometheus Books, 1994.

Quirke, Stephen. *Who Were the Pharaohs?: A History of Their Names with a List of Cartouches.* New York: Dover Publications, 1990.

Raven, J. E. *Pythagoreans and Eleatics.* Chicago: Ares Publishers, 1966.

Redford, Donald B. *Egypt, Canaan, and Israel in Ancient Times.* Princeton, NJ: Princeton University Press, 1992.

Reed, Bika. *The Field of Transformations: A Quest for the Immortal Essence of Human Awareness.* Rochester, VT: Inner Traditions International, 1987.

Reed, Bika, trans. *Rebel in the Soul: A Dialogue Between Doubt and Mystical Knowledge.* Rochester, VT: Inner Traditions International, 1978, 2nd ed. revised 1987.

Richardson, Alan, and B. Walker-John. *The Inner Guide to Egypt.* Bath, UK: Arcania Press, 1991.

Ritner, Robert Kriech. *The Mechanics of Ancient Egyptian Magical Practice.* Studies in Ancient Oriental Civilization, No. 54. Chicago: Oriental Institute of the University of Chicago, 1993.

Robins, Gay. *Proportion and Style in Ancient Egyptian Art.* Austin: University of Texas Press, 1994.

Robinson, James M., ed. *The Nag Hammadi Library.* New York: HarperSanFrancisco, 1990. 3rd ed.

Roccati, Alessandro. *Karnak and Luxor.* Egypt Classical Art Tours, ed. by Silvio Locatelli and Marcello Boroli. London: Hawk Books, n.d.

Romant, Bernard. *Life in Egypt in Ancient Times.* Trans. by J. Smith. Geneva: Minerva, 1981.

Romer, John. *Ancient Lives: Daily Life in Egypt of the Pharaohs.* New York: Holt, Rinehart and Winston, 1984.

Romilly, Jacqueline de. *A Short History of Greek Literature.* Trans. by Lillian Doherty. Chicago: University of Chicago Press, 1985.

Roth, Ann Macy. *Egyptian Phyles in the Old Kingdom: The Evolution of a System of Social Organization.* Studies in Ancient Oriental Civilization, No. 48. Chicago: Oriental Institute of the University of Chicago, 1991.

Roth, Ann Macy. "The *Pss-Kf* and the 'Opening of the Mouth' Ceremony: A Ritual of Birth and Rebirth", *Journal of Egyptian Archaeology,* pp. 113-147. 1992.

Rundle Clark, R. T. *Myth and Symbol in Ancient Egypt.* New York: Thames and Hudson, 1959.

Scott, Ernest. *The People of the Secret.* London: Octagon Press, 1983.

Scott, Walter, ed. and trans. *Hermetica: The Ancient Greek and Latin Writings Which Contain Religious or Philosophic Teachings Ascribed to Hermes Trismegistus.* Boulder, CO: Hermes House, 1982. Reprinted Boston: Shambhala, 1993.

Sellers, Jane B. *The Death of Gods in Ancient Egypt: An Essay on Egyptian Religion and the Frame of Time.* New York: Penguin Books, 1992.

Shafer, Byron E., ed. *Religion in Ancient Egypt: Gods, Myths, and Personal Practice,* by John Baines, Leonard H. Lesko, and David P. Silverman. Ithaca, NY: Cornell University Press, 1991.

Shah, Idries. *Oriental Magic.* New York: E. P. Dutton & Co., 1973.

Smith, Morton. *Jesus the Magician.* San Francisco, CA: Harper & Row, 1978.

Spencer, A. J. *Death in Ancient Egypt.* New York: Penguin Books, 1982.

Stetter, Cornelius. *The Secret Medicine of the Pharaohs: Ancient Egyptian Healing.* Chicago: Edition Q, 1993.

te Velde, H. *Seth, God of Confusion: A Study of His Role in Egyptian Mythology and Religion.* Leiden: E. J. Brill, 1977. Corrected ed.

Thorsson, Edred [= Stephen E. Flowers]. "How to be a
    Heathen" *Idunna* IV:4 (December, 1992), pp. 11-16.
Ulansey, David. *The Origins of Mithraic Mysteries: Cosmology
    and Salvation in the Ancient World.* New York: Oxford
    University Press, 1989.
Valantasis, Richard. *Spiritual Guides of the Third Century: A
    Semiotic Study of the Guide-Disciple Relationship in
    Christianity, Neoplatonism, Hermetism, and Gnosticism.*
    Harvard Dissertations in Religion No. 27. Minneapolis,
    MN: Fortress Press, 1991.
Van Gennep, Arnold. *The Rites of Passage.* Trans. by Monika
    B. Vizedom and Gabrielle L. Caffee. Chicago:
    University of Chicago Press, 1960.
Walker, Benjamin. *Gnosticism: A Concise Survey of Gnostic
    Thought from its Pre-Christian Origins to its Modern
    Manifestations.* Kent, UK: Crucible Books, 1989.
Waterfield, Robin, trans. *The Theology of Arithmetic: On the
    Mystical, Mathematical and Cosmological Symbolism of
    the First Ten Numbers.* Grand Rapids, MI: Phanes
    Press, 1988.
Wilkinson, Richard H. *Reading Egyptian Art: A Hieroglyphic
    Guide to Ancient Egyptian Painting and Sculpture.*
    New York: Thames and Hudson, 1992.

CPSIA information can be obtained at www.ICGtesting.com
Printed in the USA
BVOW08s0456240715

410092BV00003B/193/P